# MAP AND COMPASS

## About the Author

Pete Hawkins trained as a geography teacher and taught in schools for a year before escaping to the Peak District National Park's Centre for Environmental Learning for an outdoor job. As a navigation instructor, he has taught both beginners how to read a map and compass and the more experienced how to hone their navigation skills. Pete runs the Silva-sponsored Silva Navigation School.

He has written for a variety of outdoor magazines, has worked for the BBC as a local radio reporter and leads walking holidays both at home and around the world.

**Other guides by the author**
*Navigation*
*Navigating with a GPS*

# MAP AND COMPASS

## THE ART OF NAVIGATION

by
**Pete Hawkins**

2 POLICE SQUARE, MILNTHORPE, CUMBRIA, LA7 7PY
www.cicerone.co.uk

First edition 2003
ISBN 10: 1 85284 394 2
ISBN 13: 978 185284 394 6
Revised and reprinted 2005, 2006, 2008, 2010 and 2011

Printed by KHL Printing, Singapore
A catalogue record for this book is available from the British Library.
All photos by the author unless credited otherwise.

*I dedicate this book to my two wonderful children, Clare and Stephen,
who have grown up with a love for, and appreciation of, the outdoors.
You've made your old man immensely proud.*

## Acknowledgments

There are literally hundreds of people who have helped me write this book. Nearly thirty years of novice navigators who have given me the opportunity to learn the art of navigation and who constantly question me. There is always something new to stretch the grey cells and keep me on my toes. The stories and anecdotes are but a mere fraction of the ones I could have included. I thank every one of you for the fun you've given me and the many hours of laughter and interesting conversations in between the teaching.

I'd also like to thank the many colleagues I've had the privilege of working with over the years. Your influence has been immense and your commitment appreciated. Thanks to the folk at Silva UK for their support, encouragement and sponsorship over the years.

*Front cover:* Navigation away from Derwent Edge in the Peak District
*Back cover:* Remote Western Greenland – a place where good navigational skills are as essential as good equipment

# CONTENTS

# PREFACE TO THE SECOND EDITION

It would have been inconceivable back in the heady days of 1984, as I ran my very first map and compass course, that nearly thirty years later I would still be running them and have even earned a living doing so. My first book came out in 2003 and was a distillation of two decades of teaching navigation. In the intervening ten years, much has changed – not the actual navigation skills, of course, which are timeless, although I have honed both my skills and my teaching methods. The two key factors relevant to this book are the increased opportunities for walkers, with the Countryside and Rights of Way Act 2000 coming into force in the autumn of 2005, and the growing influence of technology on outdoor activities.

The CROW Act has given us vast areas of land to explore, no longer restricted to rights of way. New routes have since developed but many areas remain largely unexplored. Most outdoor enthusiasts still cling to the security blanket offered by footpaths and bridleways. Having map and compass skills and the confidence to use them will give you the freedom to step off the paths and avoid the crowds.

Ten years ago GPSs were being used in the outdoors but only in a limited way. The units were expensive and of limited accuracy. Now not only do we have more accurate GPS receivers but many come with the ability to install Ordnance Survey or other digital mapping. GPS technology is built into many smartphones, too, so the ability to walk with the aid of a pretty accurate digital locator is available to millions more who would never buy a separate GPS device.

Since 2004 I have been sponsored by Silva Ltd UK to run the Silva Navigation School. This has allowed me to immerse myself in the subject even more than I did before and this book is one result of that immersion. It takes you in a clear and practical way through the art of navigation, with a few anecdotes along the way.

It's not just aimed at walkers but relevant to any outdoor enthusiasts who want the confidence to navigate effectively and safely. Over the years I have taught horse riders, mountain bikers, mountaineers and mountain rescue personnel. This book is relevant to you all.

Writing a book is a personal odyssey – an opportunity for an author to offer his thoughts, ideas and reflections without interruption. From conversations with hundreds of readers of my previous books, I know that that journey has not been in vain, and many people are now discovering the freedom of the hills for themselves for the first time. I hope this latest book will inspire many more.

Happy reading and discovering.

*Pete Hawkins, 2012*

CHAPTER ONE

WHY LEARN
TO NAVIGATE?

# Chapter 1

*If all is not lost,
where is it?*

Anon

**W**hy learn to navigate? Are you new to walking and want to put the fundamentals of navigation in place before you try anything adventurous? Alternatively, have you been walking for a while but rely on guidebooks too much and want do your own walks? Or maybe you've been navigating for years and just want to brush up your skills. Whatever route you have followed to this book, I'm confident that your navigation skills can be revitalised and improved.

The ability to use a map and compass correctly is an important skill for all walkers but sadly many don't realise this until they need it! The usual excuse for not learning seems to be that there are plenty of guidebooks around that provide a route and a simple sketch map. One of the principal reasons for walkers signing onto my navigation courses is because they regularly get lost, despite, or maybe because, they have used a guidebook.

This book is designed to give you the skills necessary to head to the hills independently and with confidence. It will introduce the necessary skills to take you from a novice navigator to one able to cope with severe weather and tricky terrain. The first part of the book looks in detail at the map, what you need to know and what you don't, before it moves on to considering the compass. It concludes by taking a close look at the world of GPS and

*Practising map and compass skills in a group...*

digital mapping and considering the best way to incorporate these into your walking or other outdoor sport.

There are many reasons why good map and compass skills are important. Whether you spend your days on the high moors and mountains or on the lowland fields of Britain, there will be frequent occasions when these skills can make your day's walk far easier. By following your map accurately throughout the day, you can avoid getting lost – even if the weather turns bad and the mist or darkness rolls in. If you know where you are, you can stay one step ahead of trouble. A thorough knowledge of map and compass skills also gives you the freedom of the hills and the confidence to explore the UK's large areas of access land.

*...makes getting away from it all the more enjoyable*

## USEFUL NEW SKILLS

Detailed map reading can keep you out of trouble on a walk. Imagine you're on a path in arable Britain: you come to a field with shoulder-height oil seed rape and can't see which direction the path heads. By taking a bearing from the map and following it with your compass, you can navigate the field safely and legally. If you know exactly where you are, then grumbling landowners won't be able to bully and intimidate you!

Map skills are especially valuable if you're using a guidebook. Following the route on a map is far better than following a sketch map in the book. A map is more accurate and gives you a better overview of the area surrounding the walk. After all, a route in a guidebook is

*Signposts on the high moors are rare; learning to navigate is the only way*

only the author's suggestion for a good walk. With good map skills you can adapt the routes to something that better suits your needs or, better still, invent your own walks and get away from the hordes with their noses in their books.

On one occasion on the Peak District's Kinder Scout, I was stopped by a fellow walker: 'Can you tell me where we are?' he asked. 'No problem,' said I as he handed me the book he was holding. There in front of me was a guide to the Pennine Way, with the route marked on a copy of the OS map on one side of the page. Great, except the route was marked with a broad black line that obscured the relevant features marked on the map. No wonder he was lost! If he had had a proper map, things might have been different. (There are also many map-holding walkers who have got lost on Kinder. Holding a map isn't enough!)

Having the skills of navigation at your disposal is a liberating experience. Getting away from the crowds, inventing your own routes, discovering new areas and, perhaps most importantly, gaining the confidence to do it yourself is all part of making your outdoor experience more enjoyable.

## PRACTISING TECHNIQUES AND BUILDING CONFIDENCE

The joy of using a skill, like navigation, is that you will never stop learning or developing it; I'm still picking up tips and hints from people I meet. There is no one right way

*Dhulikel Sunrise, Nepal – the scenery is stunning, and the mapping is continually improving so navigation is becoming more straightforward*

of doing most of what is covered in this book and as you go through it latent memories may come back to you from your distant past, triggering memories of a technique that differs from what is given here. What is presented to you in this book are tried and tested techniques to enable you to develop your own skills. Test your methods against these and see which you prefer.

However you do it, remember that this whole process should be fun. Like any skill training, you'll discover that there are days when your understanding trundles along merrily and others when the simplest of facts refuses to go in. I advise perseverance. Take things step by step and practise as much as you can and things will fall into place. Try to find a friend you can learn with; two heads are often better than one.

This book is divided into small, easily digested sections and is designed to be read and re-read. The most essential thing you need to bring to this book is confidence. I meet folk every year who seem to get flustered when they think about navigation: 'Oh no I can't do that,' they say as they close their ears to advice. Learning to navigate is not difficult – mastering a compass involves just three straightforward steps – so relax, sit back and read on. The reward will be the freedom of the hills and the confidence to enjoy them.

# CHAPTER TWO

# INTRODUCING THE MAP

## IN THIS CHAPTER YOU'LL LEARN

- how to care for your map
- how to choose the right map for the right walk
- about map scales
- about map accuracy
- about map memory

# Chapter 2

*I lift up mine eyes to the hills, from whence cometh my help.*

The Book of Psalms 121:1

**M**aps should be the lifeblood of any walker. Understanding them is as vital as being able to put one leg in front of the other, which is why it's strange that some walkers manage to avoid them altogether. Some 'guidebook' walkers cling to their beloved tome throughout the walk, desperately poring over the text while trying to match the sketch map to the ground. Often it works but ask any of them whether they have ever got lost from following a description and most honest ones will admit they have.

Having a thorough knowledge is important, but there is more to it than that. A map is a marvellous source of information, and as you get more familiar and at ease with one, you'll find yourself spending whole evenings 'reading' them as you would a book. Maps are great and you'll soon begin to love them.

## LOOKING AFTER YOUR MAP

*A map covered with Aqua 3 will last much longer than an uncovered map and is more usable than one in a map case (Photo: Chartech International Ltd)*

Before looking at maps in detail, let's consider how to look after your map. A map is a tremendous resource and packed with lots of details. They are not cheap, however, so it is important to look after them. Even if you have a dry day, walking without some form of map cover will result in wear (and probably tear) to your map, especially around the folds. Many people use a map case and there are some excellent makes, particularly the bigger ones that allow more than just two map segments to be shown at once. There is, however, a temptation to sling the case around your neck and read the map from there. We'll talk about setting the map in the next chapter, but to briefly explain the term, it means holding the map so that the features on the map coincide with the way they appear on the ground. If the map case is slung round your neck, then you won't be doing this and you also risk death from strangulation! Getting your map out of the map case will allow you easy access to the whole of the map, especially the key.

If you want to use a map case, hold it in your hand, but if not, think about

Map shelves to be proud of

buying laminated maps. They last much longer than the paper ones and they're great for both sheltering under when it's raining and for sitting on, thus preventing DWB – damp walker's bottom!

## WHICH MAP FOR WHICH PURPOSE?

A map is a pictorial representation of the ground and the features found on it. In order to contain that information on a manageable piece of paper that information must be scaled down. A glance down the map shelves of any bookshop will reveal a wealth of maps at a variety of scales. Some are obviously aimed at pursuits other than walking. The walker who takes a road atlas onto the hills is not quite of this world or won't be for long! (Surely not, I hear you cry, who would be so foolish? Sadly, episodes such as a man clutching a road atlas trying to cross Kinder Scout from Edale to the A57 have been observed. Kinder seems to attract a high proportion of optimistic idiots!)

### What do we Mean by Scale?

#### Common Scales for Walking Maps

- 1:25,000 – 1cm on the map represents 250m on the ground

- 1:40,000 – 1cm on the map represents 400m on the ground

- 1:50,000 – 1cm on the map represents 500m on the ground

- You may also see 1:63,360. These are the old 1" to the mile maps. So, 1" on the map represents 63,360" (or 1 mile) on the ground

A scale is a ratio of distance on the map compared to distance on the ground. For example, every 1cm on the map might represent 1km on the ground. This would be a scale of 1:100,000, meaning every 1cm on the

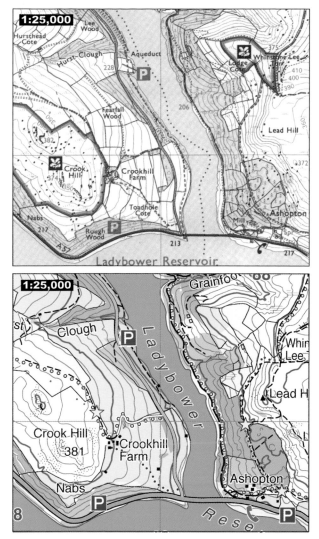

OS Explorer (top) and Harvey (left) 1:25,000 maps show field boundaries, which are very useful navigational features, as thin black lines. No distinction is made between walls, hedges, fences or ditches. Landrangers (1:50,000, below middle) do not show them.

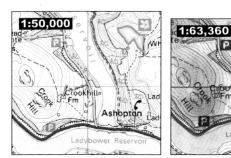

2.1 What scale map would you rather walk with?

17

map represents 100,000cm (or 1000m) on the ground. So what scale should the walker use? Consider how much a landscape changes over just a short distance. Figure 2.1 shows extracts of the same area as shown on 1:25,000, 1:40,000, 1:50,000 and 1:63,360 maps. Compare how much detail is contained on each map.

Look first at the 1:25,000 map. Follow the footpath up from the corner of the two arms of the reservoir by the number 213 (which indicates the height above sea level, but more of that later). The path starts just up from the road junction and heads uphill to a short wall, up to a wall corner (Toadhole Cote) and follows the wall side up to Crookhill Farm. Passing between the farm buildings, the path then turns east and follows the farm track down-hill to the road at the side of the reservoir. It's easy enough to follow at this scale.

Now compare that with the 1:40,000 and the 1:50,000 map. The first thing to note is the absence of walls. The path may be visible on the ground, but if it weren't how would you follow where it goes without the walls as a landmark? Once at the farm, the 1:25,000 map clearly shows the separate farm buildings and the path going between them. The 1:40,000 does indicate that the path goes between buildings but the 1:50,000 shows the exact route in much less detail. The track down to the reservoir is, however, shown.

Turning to the 1:63,360 map (the old 1″ to the mile map), the lack of detail is even greater, if that is possible. The words 'Crookhill Farm' carefully manage to obscure the details of the farm and the descending track. It is not very easy to follow this scale of map at all, though these maps did give a good overview of a large area of ground; the Peak District version covered the whole national park and were attractive to look at – but that's just about as far as they went in terms of usefulness for the outdoor enthusiast.

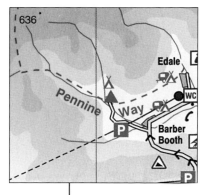

The Ordnance Survey have in fact withdrawn the 1″ series and replaced it with a 1:100,000 touring map. I mention the 1″ problem, however, because many people will still have them lying around at home. It's best to leave them there and please don't try to walk with the new touring maps. Even though the Pennine Way is marked on the Peak District map, please keep it in the car. To emphasise the point, look at Figure 2.2: would you really want to walk from this map?

*2.2 The new 1:100,000 touring map – you wouldn't really want to walk with one of these maps would you?*

Try this exercise for yourself sometime. Take an area you know well and get hold of lots of different scale maps. Go for a 'virtual' walk and compare the level of detail on the different maps.

## The Useful Scales

Back to the useful scales: a 1:25,000 map scale means that every 1cm on the map represents 25,000cm on the ground or, to put it in a different way, 1cm on the map represents 250m on the ground. A 1:50,000 map scales down 500m on the ground to 1cm on the map.

The old excuse for not using 1:25,000 maps was that they were mostly on small sheets so any decent walk would require two or three maps. Now that the Ordnance Survey have brought out the Explorer map series this is no longer the case (these have replaced the old second series green-covered maps and the yellow-covered Outdoor Leisure maps). Every area of the UK is now covered by an Explorer map and there are no more excuses; the scale for outdoor use is 1:25,000.

That is not to say that 1:50,000 maps aren't useful. In some hilly areas the shape of the ground is such that the contours on the map are close enough together to show the land's shape well. Figure 2.3 illustrates this well. You can 'see' the shape of the ground clearly from the contours. Take your 1:50,000 map out for a walk occasionally and see how you get on. At the very least it will give

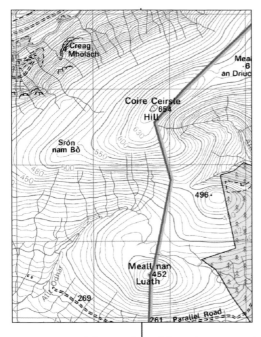

2.3 On hilly ground 1:50,000 contours show the shape of the ground well

2.4 Harvey maps: they may look different but they're still an excellent resource for hillwalkers

you practice in using a different map scale, and that is an important skill, especially if you intend walking abroad.

## MAKING MAPS

As the country's national mapping agency, the Ordnance Survey (OS) (a financially independent government agency), was, for years, the sole producer of quality maps. The standards set by the OS cartographers are those against which other maps are judged. They aren't alone any more though. Harvey Map Services sprang onto the scene a few years ago with their unusually scaled 1:40,000 (1cm on the map represents 400m on the ground). These maps looked very different to OS maps and took a while to be accepted as a result. The colour scheme was based on that used for orienteering maps (their latest maps use a 'toned down' (in Harvey's own words) version of these colours).

Harvey have now become a regular feature on the hills and have been the maps of choice for many of the big mountain marathon events. The company has now brought out the 1:25,000 scale Superwalker maps. These are only produced for major upland areas but are

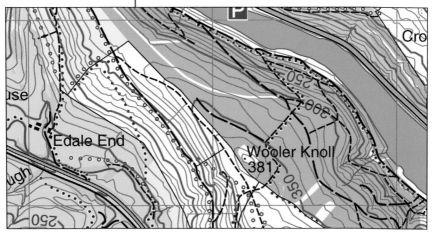

excellent alternatives to the OS maps. They also have a growing series of maps that cover the long-distance trails, that could save you from having to carry lots of OS maps. More recently Harvey produced the British Mountain Map series with the British Mountaineering Council and the British Geological Survey back at the 1:40,000 scale. (See Figure 2.4 for an extract.)

Compare these map extracts showing Kinder Scout (Figure 2.5). They look different and emphasise some features differently (especially the water) but this doesn't mean that one is better or worse than the other.

Some walkers take up orienteering to help develop their map and compass skills. The scale of orienteering maps typically varies from 1:15,000 down to 1:5000. Check with the map before setting off for a 'run' so you know what scale you are using! It's a good tip; it is very easy to overestimate how far you've got to go, thus missing the next marker disastrously. Navigation book writers have even been known to get this wrong!

(Orienteering is mentioned again in Chapter 12. Details of how to contact the British Orienteering Federation can be found in Appendix A.)

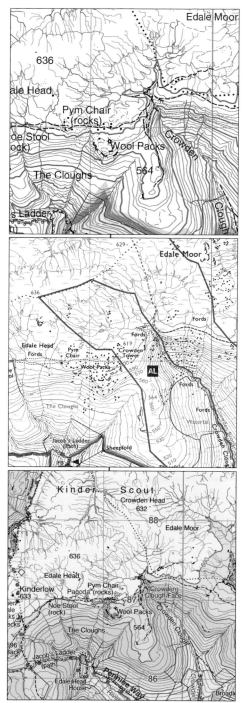

*2.5 Kinder Scout as shown (top to bottom) on a 1:25,000 Harvey Superwalker, 1:25,000 OS Explorer and a BMC 1:40,000 Mountain Map (made by Harvey)*

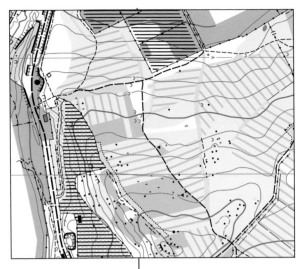

## HOW ACCURATE IS A MAP?

There is a misconception among some map users that maps are 100% accurate. Just consider how much the fringes of our urban areas have changed over recent years – OS surveyors spend most of their time in such locations. Some landscapes will alter little, but even rural locations undergo changes, and if maps are only updated on an irregular basis you must assume that there will be elements of a map that will be wrong.

On the beginner navigation courses I teach, we take over an hour to get out of the village. That's not because they're all rubbish, it's because we spend our time really looking at the fine details on the map. In doing so we quickly discover that the map is not just wrong occasionally but frequently. Figure 2.6d shows part of the walk and shows just how much of the map is wrong. At point A, the house on the left-hand side of the road (2.6a), that has been there since 1977, was still not on the map in 2011. Point B (2.6b), the newish (five years ago) extension to the housing estate was also not shown and at point C a wall was shown running through the 'L' of Lane on the map (2.6c) but one of the two parallel walls has now gone! (The 2012 version of the map, published while this guide was being written, has finally acknowledged the housing estate.)

However enough is right with the map that by studying the detail you can still accurately locate yourself and not be phased by seeing something that is on the ground and not on the map or vice versa. Beware, however, that if you don't look at the map closely, it is possible to get lost by moving yourself on to a point on the map which 'fits' what you see better than you actual location – this is a frequent cause of getting lost.

### Map Memory

Memorising what is coming ahead will help cut down on errors; having a 'map memory' is an important part of a navigator's skills.

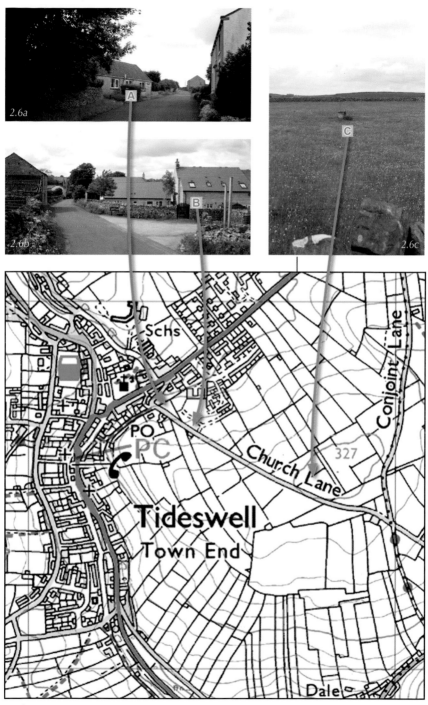

2.6a

2.6b

2.6c

2.6d

Take out a local 1:25,000 map to a reasonably complicated area – the edge of a village for example. Look at the fine detail of the map and compare it with what you see on the ground. How accurate is it? (You may find that using your compass's magnifying lens is helpful here.) See whether you can find as many errors as I have in 2.6 above.

It may seem slightly daunting at this stage to casually say 'develop a map memory', but the more you use maps, the more you study them and understand the symbols, then the more likely you are to develop the ability to remember what the map looks like for short sections at a time.

When we go for a walk in a familiar location we subconsciously use landmarks to navigate by. To illustrate this, just describe to yourself a short walk from your house, to your nearby pub for example, as though you were describing the route to someone who didn't know where they were going. You'd be using phrases like, 'cross the road when you get to the post box' or 'turn left at the butcher's and then right when you get to the next road junction'. This use of landmarks is an important part of navigation and one you need to create artificially if you aren't familiar with an area.

Figure 2.7 shows a small section of the Lake District. If we start at Thrushwood (A) and going to Applethwaite (B), what kind of thing should you be looking at to help you develop your map memory?,

Leaving the road, we cross the small strip of woodland and take the path along a field boundary and into the next field. The actual right of way starts on the eastern side of the field and then, towards the top, you cross the field towards the buildings (landmark 1). The next field is a large one with Ormathwaite Hall at the top. Look at the contours. While we're climbing it's only gentle as they are well spread out. The next landmark (2) is the end of the field boundary we're following, the track continues in the same direction but at this point we must turn left with the field boundary. Our next landmark to tick off

Go for a short walk and divide the walk up into short sections, say 1km at a time. At the start of each section, look at the map and try to memorise the features you see on it. Tick these features off when you get to them and move onto the next one.

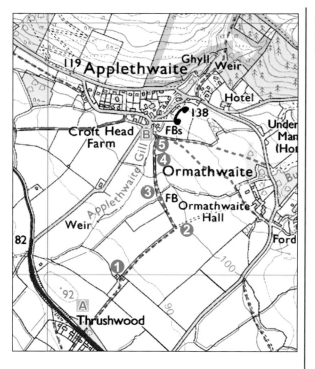

2.7 Memorising what you'll walk past will help your navigation

Mist over Lose Hill, in the Peak District

is the footbridge over the stream (landmarks). The path then gently bends north and eventually runs parallel to Applethwaite Gill (landmark 4) before a path joins us from the right and we cross the last footbridge (landmark 5) and enter Applethwaite.

As you continue through this book, you may begin to wonder how you'll manage to remember all the things mentioned. If you drive you probably had the same thought during your first few driving lessons: 'How will I manage to look in the mirror, change gear, press the clutch and sing along with the tape all at the same time?' Once you pass, you quickly develop your skills to enable you to do all that and look at the scenery simultaneously. The same will happen with your map-reading skills.

Over the coming chapters, the skills you'll need to master both the map and compass will be analysed. First, the map will be examined in more detail and some of the squiggly lines and symbols that cover it will be dissected.

## Key Points

- Use a map case or a laminated map.
- The scale on a map is a ratio of map distance to ground distance, so 1:25,000 means 1 map centimetre represents 250m on the ground.
- The best scale for walkers' maps is 1:25,000.
- Get familiar with using maps of different scales from different makers.
- Maps are never 100% accurate.
- Try to develop a map memory.

# MAP DETAIL

## IN THIS CHAPTER YOU'LL LEARN

- the different map symbols and know which are important and which aren't
- the difference between a path and a right of way
- when a path becomes a track
- how rights of way get put on maps
- about permissive, or concessionary, paths
- about long-distance trails and cycle ways
- about access land and access laws in England, Scotland, Ireland and Wales
- the difference between the different types of map symbols
- how much detail is contained on a map

# Chapter 3

*The hardest thing to see is
what is in front of your eyes*

Johann Wolfgang von
Goethe

Many people I teach say they can read a map, but after spending a while with them it transpires that their knowledge is often superficial. A map contains a tremendous amount of detail and an ability to understand and be able to act on that detail is important. However, it is also important to know which symbols you can ignore because they don't describe observable objects: how many people have followed a parish boundary thinking it was a footpath?

To develop this further, let's consider briefly and simply how the Ordnance Survey draw up their maps. First they survey an area aerially and then, using old maps, current images and a clever cartographer, they draw up the new version. If a path goes onto the map at this stage, it is because it is visible on the ground and is therefore shown by black pecks. With the first draft finished, the OS send it to the relevant highways authority who then take out their green pen and mark on all the public rights of way. The footpath officer for the local group of the Ramblers' Association is also consulted. The map comes back to the OS and the final version is produced, with public rights of way shown by green dashes and other paths as black pecks.

Take a look at the key on an Ordnance Survey 1:25,000 Explorer map. You'll see that it's divided up it into several sections. We'll look at some of these and consider which are important to walkers and which are less so. Let's start at the top.

## MAP SYMBOLS

### Roads, Paths and Public Rights of Way
Figure 3.1 shows all the symbols used to show lines of communication, whether you are travelling by foot, car or train. With roads, generally speaking, the more important a road is, the larger it is drawn and the more obvious the colours used. Most of the road symbols can be ignored, but if you want peace and quiet when walking, plan a walk that avoids them! Paths are shown on maps (the short black dashes or 'pecks' as the OS call them) and public rights of way are also shown (green dashes). The existence of a path on the ground does not mean it is a right of way unless it is both marked with a black dash and a green dash together. Look closely at any 1:25,000

## ROADS AND PATHS    Not necessarily rights of way

Ⓢ    Service area

7    Junction number

M I or A 6(M)    Motorway

A 35    Dual carriageway

A 30    Main road

B 3074    Secondary road

Narrow road with passing places

Road under construction

Road generally more than 4 m wide

Road generally less than 4 m wide

Other road, drive or track, fenced and unfenced

Gradient: steeper than 20% (1 in 5);   14% (1 in 7) to 20% (1 in 5)

Ferry    Ferry; Ferry P - passenger only

Path

## RAILWAYS

Multiple track ⎫ standard
Single track ⎭ gauge

Narrow gauge or
Light rapid transit system (LRTS) and station

Road over; road under; level crossing

Cutting; tunnel; embankment

Station, open to passengers; siding

## PUBLIC RIGHTS OF WAY    (Rights of way are not shown on maps of Scotland)

Footpath
Bridleway
Byway open to all traffic
Restricted byway
(not for use by mechanically propelled vehicles)

Public rights of way shown on this map have been taken from local authority definitive maps and later amendments.
Rights of way are liable to change and may not be clearly defined on the ground.
Please check with the relevant local authority for the latest information

**The representation on this map of any other road, track or path is no evidence of the existence of a right of way**

*3.1 Extracts from the key of the OS Explorer 1:25,000 map*

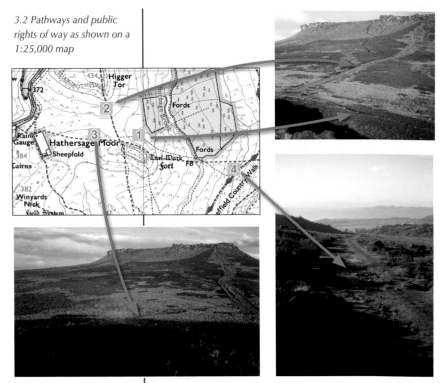

3.2 Pathways and public rights of way as shown on a 1:25,000 map

map and you'll see many examples. (Further information about access is given below.)

Figure 3.2 shows a small map extract. This has both black and green dashes, some coinciding and some not. Let's consider what is going on here.

### Paths and Tracks

The black dashes denote that a path is visible on the ground. (Path 1 is one example.) However, as Path 1 doesn't have a green dash above it, it is not a public right of way and could have been made by livestock. Path 2 consists of both black and green dashes: there is a path visible on the ground and it is a right of way. Path 3 is a right of way (indicated by the green dashed line) but there isn't a path visible on the ground. Path 4 is different. You'll notice the markings used here consist of two parallel dashes: these denote a track. (A track is wider than a path and is usually made by vehicles – however it is not is necessarily a right of way. Only if there is a green dash above the track, as in Path 4, has it been identified as a right of way.) If one of the dashed lines were solid, then

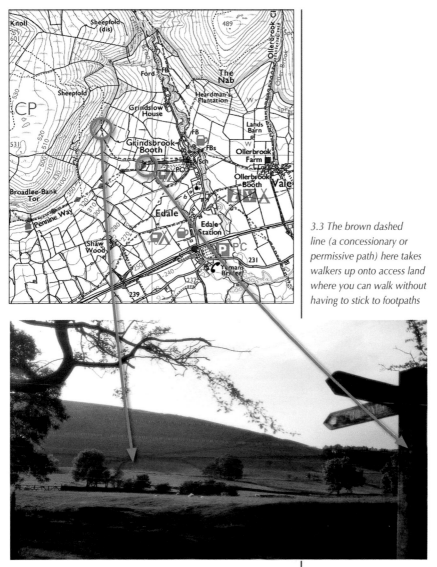

3.3 The brown dashed line (a concessionary or permissive path) here takes walkers up onto access land where you can walk without having to stick to footpaths

you'd have a fence, wall or hedge on that side of the track; if both were solid there would be a physical boundary on both sides. The green dashes on this map are short ones, denoting a footpath; longer green dashes would indicate a bridleway (open to horses, cyclists and walkers).

## Other Rights of Way

There are other rights of way symbols in the key: byways open to all traffic (cars and motorbikes as well

*Because walkers are charged to walk this route on one day a year, this path can't be designated a public right of way...*

*...and other activities can then take place*

*3.4 The green circles denote an 'other route with public access' – here they follow a track. The brown circles show an off-route cycle route which is also a permissive path (brown dashes).*

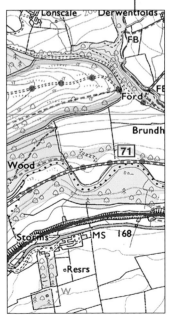

as pedestrians and cyclists) and restricted byways (previously known as 'roads used as public paths' – with the wonderful acronym RUPPs – but now re-designated along with a change in the type of users who can use them). The only losers here will be those people who used their four-wheelers or scramble bikes on RUPPs, as the new restricted byways are available only to walkers, horse riders, cyclists and drivers of horse-drawn vehicles.

There are also other kinds of paths open to walkers. Permissive or concessionary paths are shown by brown dashes (Figure 3.3 and Figure 3.4); the short dashes represent permissive footpaths and the longer dashes show permissive bridleways. A permissive right of way is a route that the landowner has given the public permission to use, without it being a public right of way. The fact that you can walk along it one day doesn't necessarily mean that you can the next: the path may be closed for game shooting or, at certain times of year, to protect ground-nesting birds. This is perfectly legal and any restrictions in force will normally be posted on a nearby sign. Very often farmers will open a permissive footpath as an alternative to a path going through the farmyard, again a perfectly acceptable alternative, in my opinion, so long as the new path is in good condition and is well signed.

**RIGHTS OF WAY & ACCESS**

Information supplied by Peak District National Park

ᴸ·ᴸ·ᴸ  Public footpath with path on the ground

·····  Public footpath without path on the ground

ₒ·ₒ·ₒ  Public bridleway with path on the ground

ₒ ₒ ₒ ₒ  Public bridleway without path on the ground

ₒ ₒ ₒ ₒ  Permissive path (permission may be withdrawn)

◻  Public access land (land open to the public with permission of the landowners. This may be withdrawn)

■ ■ ■  Boundary not confirmed

◻  National Trust access land (always open)

*3.5 Rights of way as shown on a Harvey map*

There are also situations where local agreements mean that a regularly used path can't become a public right of way. Lathkill Dale in Derbyshire is a case in point: once a year Natural England collects 20p from passing walkers. As long as they do this, the path will never become a right of way. This state of affairs allows the owners to close it for their own purposes (in Lathkill's case, the Haddon Estates own and shoot on the land).

Rights of way are only shown in green on the OS 1:25,000 map. On a 1:50,000, they are shown in red and permissive paths aren't shown at all. The Harvey maps are different again, as shown in Figure 3.4.

## Other Public Access

There are other route symbols worth mentioning here. Green diamonds denote a national trail, long-distance footpath or a recreational route; examples include the Pennine Way or the Coast-to-Coast path, but could also include shorter routes set up by the local authority to encourage folk into the countryside. Brown dots are 'off road cycle routes' and green dots denote other routes with public access. Figure 3.4 shows both brown and green dotted routes and a couple of permissive routes.

Finally, before we leave the discussion of rights of way, we need to take a brief look at permission. Occasionally, while out on the hills, you may be passed by people riding scrambling bikes along your path. As they're not permitted, except on bridleways, you might feel like leaping out in front of them to prevent them passing. However, if the owner of the land through which you are passing has given his permission to these riders, there is little you

## OTHER PUBLIC ACCESS

● ● ●     Other routes with public access (not normally shown in urban areas)

The exact nature of the rights on these routes and the existence of any restrictions may be checked with the local highway authority. Alignments are based on the best information available

◆   ◆     🔔 National Trail / (👣) Long Distance Route   ◆   ◆   Recreational Route

---- --------     Permissive footpath ⎤   Footpaths and bridleways along which
    landowners have permitted public use
    but which are not rights of way.
— — — —     Permissive bridleway ⎦   The agreement may be withdrawn

● ● ●     Traffic-free cycle route

[1]   National cycle network route number - traffic free     ▮1   National cycle network route number - on road

### Scotland

In Scotland, everyone has access rights in law* over most land and inland water, provided access is exercised responsibly. **This includes walking, cycling, horse-riding and water access, for recreational and educational purposes, and for crossing land or water.** Access rights do not apply to motorised activities, hunting, shooting or fishing, nor if your dog is not under proper control. The **Scottish Outdoor Access Code** is the reference point for responsible behaviour, and can be obtained at **www.outdooraccess-scotland.com** or by phoning your local Scottish Natural Heritage office.   *Land Reform (Scotland) Act 2003

🔲 🔲     National Trust for Scotland, always open / limited opening - observe local signs

🔲 🔲     Forestry Commission Land / Woodland Trust Land

### England & Scotland

▶ DANGER AREA     Firing and test ranges in the area. Danger! Observe warning notices
Champs de tir et d'essai. Danger! Se conformer aux avertissements
Schiess und Erprobungsgelände. Gefahr! Warnschilder beachten
Visit **www.access.mod.uk** for information

*Other public access symbols from an OS Explorer map*

can do to stop them. For an excellent little (free) booklet on rights in the country call Natural England (0845 600 3078) and ask for their *Out in the Country* booklet CA9 (ISBN: 0 86170 609 9) or in Wales call the Countryside Council for Wales on 0845 130 6229.

## MAPS AS HISTORICAL RECORDS

Do bear in mind what was said in the last chapter: a map is a historical record. The fact that a path is shown as a legal right of way on a map does not necessarily mean that it still is one. Of course, any alteration to the network should be well signed on the ground and if this is the case then follow the signage and not the map. If there are no recent signposts or any obvious well-maintained re-routing that suggests an alternative route, it is best to believe the map.

A few years ago, as part of a map and compass series in a magazine, I was asked to detail my thought processes when I plan a route. So, rather than choosing an area I knew very well, I planned a route on Dartmoor. A few months later I found myself on Dartmoor and decided to walk my route. All was going well until I got to the way-side cross. The route then went on a bearing into thick mist to a track on the moor top. Could it be found? I did everything I could think of to find it, including most of the techniques included in later chapters. After walking that stretch three or four times I finally stopped where I thought the track should be. Out came the flask and I sat down to ponder. I looked at the map and the key (it was a Harvey map) and eventually unfolded the whole map to spot a little sentence: 'Ancient travel route no longer definable on ground'!

I couldn't help wondering how many people had taken my route and tried to walk it only to discover this same problem. (You'll be pleased to know the rest of the walk went fine!)

*OK Hawkins, here's the cross, so where's the track?*

## LAWS OF ACCESS AND RIGHTS OF WAY

The law concerning rights of way is complicated and has kept the legal bodies of many a local authority and the Ramblers' Association busy for years. With the further complication that the Countryside and Rights of Way Act has re-defined access and rights of way, it's perhaps worthwhile spending time considering the situation in Great Britain.

### Access and Rights of Way in England and Wales

When the law changed in 2000, much of where walkers were allowed to go didn't change: for example, footpath rights weren't altered. Natural England has a useful summary in a leaflet entitled *Countryside Access and the new rights* summarising where walkers can walk, download-able from their website. The list, subject to local conditions, includes footpaths, bridleways and byways, public open spaces (like parks), most beaches and towpaths, much common land, land under access agreements, some woods and forests, open country and coastline owned by the National Trust and the National Cycle Network.

Where the Act was radical was in establishing the 'right to roam' on mountains, moorlands, downland and heaths. Since the Act became law in 2000, there has been a great deal of debate about what this includes, but September 2004 saw the Act enabled in the first two areas (Lower North West and South East England). The rest of the country came under the Act during 2005. The result is that there is now substantially more countryside across which we can wander at will. Those with map and compass skills are now able to make full use of these new freedoms. Local restrictions apply, but these are well signed and marked on maps.

Bear in mind, however, that the new Act only applies to England and Wales; the situation in Scotland and Ireland is different and more complicated.

### Access in Scotland

Scottish access is an issue that has confused many a walker venturing into the Scottish hills, so it was a welcome relief when the Land Reform (Scotland) Act was passed in 2003. This Act, among other things, created a right of 'responsible access to land' which formally legislated for what has existed without legislation in Scotland for many years. It establishes a public right of responsible access to land, including inland waterways, for both educational and recreational purposes. It also requires that

*Leaflets like this are useful; they tell you what you can and can't do in the countryside*

landowners ensure that such access rights can be reason-ably exercised.

The issues surrounding rights of way are separate from those linked with the freedom to roam. Scottish rights of way were developed in the 19th century when the estates that were organising shooting parties wanted to stop the public using passes and routes they had walked for years in order to hunt the land undisturbed. In the end a number of paths were given specific legal protection and became rights of way. To many these undermine the con-cept of the freedom to roam. What confuses many who don't walk often in Scotland is that rights of way are not shown on OS maps. However, so long as walkers behave responsibly, access to paths marked on maps shouldn't be a problem.

There are early plans for putting what the Scots are calling 'Core Paths' (paths in and around towns and cities) onto maps, but this won't happen for a number of years yet. For more details about access in Scotland and the Scottish Outdoor Access Code, see the Scottish Natural Heritage website www.snh.org.uk.

*The Southern Upland Way, an obvious right of way in Scotland*

## Ireland

The situation in both Northern Ireland and Eire is again different and far from clear. There are long-distance trails that, in part, go over privately owned mountains and moorlands but, as there isn't a history of public footpaths and rights of access, the access tends to depend on the kindness of the landowner. The best advice if you are planning a walk in Ireland is to seek guidance from the nearest tourist information centre.

The moors offer wide open
spaces and freedom

Access land sign in England
and Wales

## GENERAL INFORMATION

### Access Land

Access land is the bread and butter of an able navigator: here you can wander at will without having to stick to footpaths. There are numerous bylaws that affect what walkers can and can't do on access land, including preaching sermons! However most are common sense (including preaching). The most important thing about access land is that it offers just that, access; and this is where good navigation skills are essential. Before the CROW Act, access used to be depicted by purple boundary lines with a purple arrow showing access points. Since the Act was enabled in 2004 and 2005, the new maps show a different set of symbols. Access land is now tinted light yellow with a orange band at the edge. Access land in woodland is shaded a lighter green than non access woodland, and access information points are a white 'i' in an orange circle. The new symbols make it much easier to work out where access land is. (Access land will have rights of way crossing it but, as I've said, the point is that you don't have to stick to them.)

The pre-CROW Act maps used to show access land owned by organisations like the National Trust and Woodland Trust with their own symbols. These are no longer shown on the new maps; all access land is depicted using the new shading.

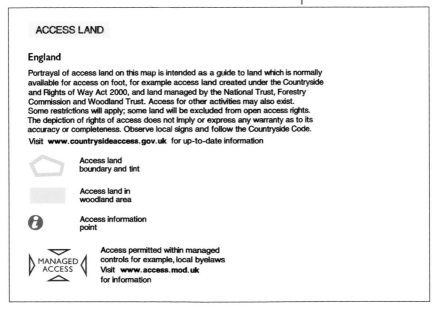

**ACCESS LAND**

Land open to the public by permission of the owners. The agreement may be withdrawn

National Trust, always open

National Trust, limited access - observe local signs

National Trust for Scotland, always open

National Trust for Scotland, limited access - observe local signs

Forestry Commission

Woodland Trust

Other access land

Access information point

DANGER AREA

Firing and test ranges in the area. Danger! Observe warning notices
Champs de tir et d'essai. Danger! Se conformer aux avertissements
Schiess und Erprobungsgelände. Gefahr! Warnschilder beachten

As has been said, there are numerous laws and bylaws governing access land. One focuses on providing regulation for closure of access land. The landowner has the right to exclude or restrict the new access rights for up to 28 days a year, excluding public holidays, and for a maximum of four weekends, for any reason, as long as the relevant authority is informed.

*Access land symbols on Explorer maps that pre-date the implementation of the CROW Act*

Reasons for closures will vary, but it may be for game shooting or when land-owners wish to carry out land management work. Access land can also be closed when there are exceptional fire risks too.

*The current access land symbols on Explorer maps*

**ACCESS LAND**

**England**

Portrayal of access land on this map is intended as a guide to land which is normally available for access on foot, for example access land created under the Countryside and Rights of Way Act 2000, and land managed by the National Trust, Forestry Commission and Woodland Trust. Access for other activities may also exist. Some restrictions will apply; some land will be excluded from open access rights. The depiction of rights of access does not imply or express any warranty as to its accuracy or completeness. Observe local signs and follow the Countryside Code.
Visit **www.countrysideaccess.gov.uk** for up-to-date information

Access land boundary and tint

Access land in woodland area

Access information point

MANAGED ACCESS

Access permitted within managed controls for example, local byelaws
Visit **www.access.mod.uk** for information

These closures don't affect public rights of way, however. A right of way can only be closed to control the spread of animal diseases like foot and mouth. Again, the *Countryside Access and the new rights* booklet is a good source of further information.

Similar to access land is land designated as Environmental Stewardship land. Stewardship is a scheme set up by Natural England to encourage landowners to farm in a more environmentally sensitive way. Part of the agreement is that the public should have open access to the land. Stewardship land is only shown on maps where the agreement is for longer than 20 years. The OS says that if land under shorter agreements were shown, the map could date too quickly. There is, however, a website that shows where Environmental Stewardship land is: www.cwr.naturalengand.org.uk.

## MORE MAP SYMBOLS

### General Features
Once you have sussed out the path network on your maps you should begin to learn other symbols. Maps have three types of symbol:

*General features symbols on Explorer maps*

- symbols showing the location of a feature (like a church)
- symbols to show the approximate area that a feature may be in (for example a tree symbol)
- symbols for features that don't appear on the ground (such as a parish boundary).

---

### GENERAL FEATURES

|  |  |
|---|---|
| + | Place of worship |
| Current or former place of worship | with tower |
|  | with spire, minaret or dome |
| ▢ ▢ | Building; important building |
| ▨ | Glasshouse |
| ▲ | Youth hostel |
| ■ | Bunkhouse/camping barn/other hostel |
| ⬤ | Bus or coach station |
| ⚲ ⚲ ⚲ | Lighthouse; disused lighthouse; beacon |
| △ ⊤ | Triangulation pillar; mast |
| ⚵ | Windmill, with or without sails |
| ⚵ ⚵ | Wind pump; wind turbine |
| pylon  pole | Electricity transmission line |
| ⅏⅏⅏ | Slopes |

|  |  |  |  |
|---|---|---|---|
| ⬭ | Gravel pit | ⬭ | Sand pit |
| ⬭ | Other pit or quarry | ⬭ | Landfill site or slag/spoil heap |
| BP/BS | Boundary post/stone | | |
| CG | Cattle grid | | |
| CH | Clubhouse | | |
| FB | Footbridge | | |
| MP; MS | Milepost ; milestone | | |
| Mon | Monument | | |
| PO | Post office | | |
| Pol Sta | Police station | | |
| Sch | School | | |
| TH | Town hall | | |
| NTL | Normal tidal limit | | |
| W; Spr | Well; spring | | |

Lighthouse; disused lighthouse; beacon

Triangulation pillar; mast

3.6 They may be similar
sizes in the key...

Whether the feature is visible and accurately located or not, it is worthwhile pointing out something that may seem obvious: the size of the symbol does not have to correlate with its actual size on the ground. Consider a 1:25,000 map, which means that every 1cm on the map represents 250m on the ground. This divides further so 1mm on the map represents 25m on the ground. Look at the symbol for a triangulation pillar and for a windmill. The two symbols are drawn to roughly the same size but in reality (Figure 3.6) they are rather different!

Archaeological and historical information and general feature symbols marked on the map are physical 'objects' that you will find on the ground. Boundaries generally won't be visible and single vegetation symbols are used to denote areas covered by a particular type of vegetation: you will, for example, find a wood where a tree symbol is, rather than a single tree.

Other symbols will be considered later on, but one question often asked is, 'How do I learn all that lot?' Experience has shown me that the best way to learn is to practise. Take your map out on a familiar walk. We all have a walk we do often, even if it's a circuit round the park with the dog. It is a rare individual who takes a map out with them on every occasion but, by doing so, you can compare the familiar features on the ground with the way they are displayed on the map. In the end you'll become familiar with those symbols without even trying. The first time I took my

...but they're
not on the ground!

own advice, I was surprised just how much I had missed. It was on a walk I'd done many times up onto the Lose Hill ridge in the Peak District. Once the map came with me I discovered all sorts of unnoticed features and rarely used paths. It doubled my enjoyment of the walk and gave me many new options for the future.

Take your map out on other less familiar walks too and you'll soon realise that you know most of the symbols by heart. When you go into a new area then you'll only have a few extra symbols to learn. I don't often do coastal walks so I don't know the coastal symbols by heart, but when I do it doesn't take long to learn the extra ones I need.

If you really are forgetful, take a map, cut the key out, laminate it and keep it handy on your walk; you won't have to unfold your map every time something foxes you.

## LOOKING IN DETAIL

It is important to realise that there is a great deal of detail on a map. Few newcomers to navigation examine maps in enough detail. This means they fail to understand everything that a map shows and how it can be used to help them navigate. Practising looking at the minute details on a map and seeing what they look like on the ground will ensure that you develop an understanding of how the map relates to the ground. From this strong foundation you will be able later on to learn and apply more advanced navigation techniques (see Chapters 11 and 12) that will be useful on those days when the visibility on the hills is poor.

Figure 3.7 shows a rectangle taken from a map with an enlarged version of the same rectangle positioned below it. The plan is to walk from the corner of the road (above where it says 'Sch'), up the path, behind Birchover, to the next road. Looking closely at the map, you can see the start of the walk is just round the bend, away from the village (Photo A). The path goes to the left of a small enclosure, and then up the corner of a wall, where another path crosses the one you're on (Photo B). The path follows the wall on the right for a while, before leaving it behind (where it says Barton Hill Quarries). The shading indicates that you're walking through woodland at this point. Further up (just after the words), the path joins a track, shown by the two pairs of parallel dashes (Photo C). On the right

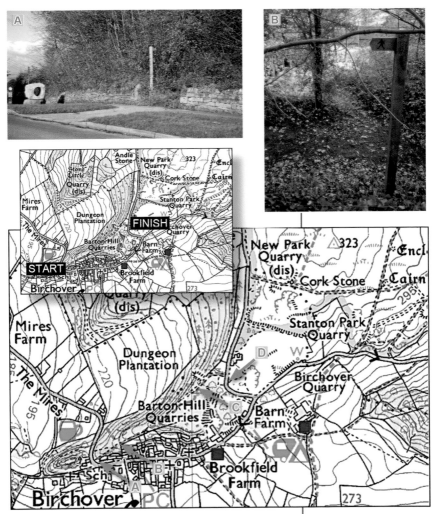

3.7 There's a great deal of detail on maps

there are quarries and embankments. Just before the path hits the road, it swings right; there appears to be a building on the other side of the road. Over to your left as you head to the road is a walled enclosure, which turns out to be a car park (Photo D).

Looking at a map in this sort of detail is a worthwhile skill to develop, especially when you start map reading. How many times have you started a walk and gone in the wrong direction? Spending a couple of minutes studying the map in detail, especially if you are in a complicated location like a village where there is a lot going on, will help to prevent this happening. Not only will you be able to match the features shown on the map with their real life counterparts but you'll also be able to set the map at the same time.

Once studying the map in close detail becomes second nature, you'll be able to spot features along your walk that you can tick off mentally as you go. It can also help when negotiating a tricky part of the map, say through a farmyard, where accuracy is important. The whole exercise also displays just what level of detail you can get from a map. Try a similar exercise yourself sometime.

## Key Points

- Paths and tracks are not necessarily rights of way.
- Permissive, or concessionary, paths can be walked on but that right can be taken away if the landowner so chooses.
- Access laws in England, Wales, Scotland and Ireland are different and complicated.
- Access land allows you to walk off rights of way.
- Some symbols on maps relate to features you won't see on the ground.
- Learn to look at the detail of a map: it'll make you a more accurate navigator.

# CHAPTER FOUR

# GRIDLINES AND REFERENCES

## IN THIS CHAPTER YOU'LL LEARN ABOUT

- the National Grid Reference System
- grid letters
- four-figure grid references
- six-figure grid references (and more)
- Romers
- setting the map
- thumbing

# Chapter 4

If you don't know where
you are going, all
roads lead there.

Roman proverb

Having studied the symbols and had some practice looking at the detail of the map, let's take a slight step back and look at another important set of symbols, marked on a map and not visible on the ground – grid lines.

## THE NATIONAL GRID

Take a look at an OS map and you will notice the parallel vertical and horizontal lines that cover the map – grid lines. These lines are blue on a 1:25,000 map and black on a 1:50,000 OS map. Using these lines enables us to give an accurate reference for any location on the map.

They are numbered in ascending order from left to right for the vertical lines and bottom to top for the horizontal ones. The numbering starts at zero and runs up to 99. Why? I'll come back to that later. Much as you would have done as a child when you played battleships you can give locations on the map a unique grid reference by combining the horizontal numbers with the vertical ones. Let's look at a practical example.

Figure 4.1 shows a section of map showing a church with a tower. Imagine we were starting our walk there and needed to give people a grid reference so they could find it. Looking at the diagram we can see the brown square in question lies in between the 05 and 06 vertical lines and the 33 and 34 horizontal lines. Always go for the lower of the two numbers, so the grid reference – the so-called four-figure reference – is 05 33. Figure 4.2 shows why; the yellow shading shows the section of the map that would have 05 in the reference and the blue shading the area with the 33. The square with both is our 05 33 square in question.

If you are looking for a way to remember how to read grid references then all you need to remember is the saying 'Along the corridor and up the stairs'? To translate this into grid references, read the numbers along the top or bottom of the map first – going along the corridor, followed by the ones up the side – up the stairs. These numbers are given fancy names on maps which I personally think are confusing – eastings (numbers get higher the further east you go) and northings (numbers rise as you go north). It is far easier to remember to go along the corridor and up the stairs.

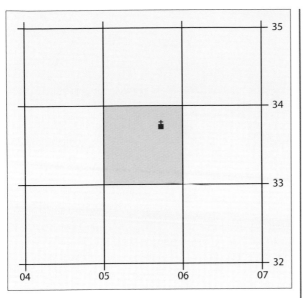

4.1 Reading four-figure grid references

Let's change the church to a pub and tell our friends we'll meet them at the pub at 05 33. We tell our friends where the walk starts and we think we're done. However, as Figure 4.3 shows, there are pubs in both squares and they both have the same four-figure grid reference of 05 33. Now the one on the left is from the Derby Explorer map 259 and the one on the right is from the

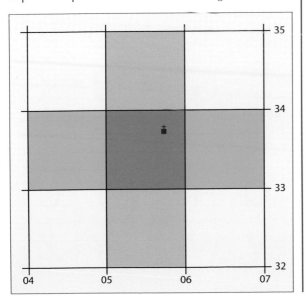

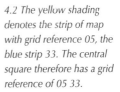

4.2 The yellow shading denotes the strip of map with grid reference 05, the blue strip 33. The central square therefore has a grid reference of 05 33.

47

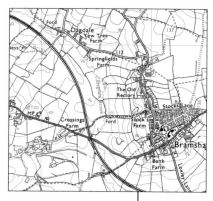

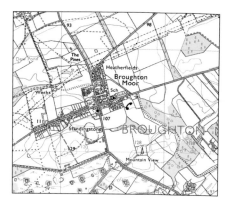

*4.3 Two squares with the grid reference 05 33*

North-Western Lakes (OL4) map. It is unlikely that your friends will end up at the wrong pub but there are plenty of instances where being able to identify the correct square is important. It's here we need to step back and take a look at the bigger picture, in this case the whole of Great Britain.

Figure 4.4 shows Great Britain overlaid by 25 large squares, 500 by 500km, lettered from A to Z (omitting the letter I). Britain lies roughly in the centre under the squares N, S, H and T. These individual large squares are further broken down to 25 smaller squares lettered A to Z (again, omitting I), as shown in the large square B. The size of these squares is 100 by 100km. These smaller

*4.4 The 500km² grid system with the smaller sub-divisions © Crown Copyright*

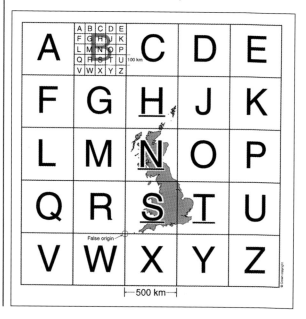

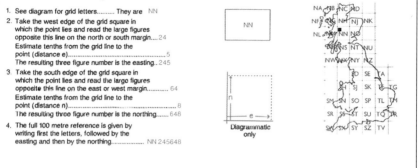

## THE NATIONAL GRID REFERENCE SYSTEM

Base map constructed on Transverse Mercator Projection, Airy Spheroid, OSGB (1936) Datum. Vertical datum mean sea level (Newlyn).

The grid lines form part of the national grid and are at 1 km intervals.
To give a unique reference defining the position of a point to within 100 metres proceed as follows:-

EXAMPLE    Locheilt Lodge

1. See diagram for grid letters.......... They are   NN
2. Take the west edge of the grid square in
   which the point lies and read the large figures
   opposite this line on the north or south margin.... 24
   Estimate tenths from the grid line to the
   point (distance e)..................................... 5
   The resulting three figure number is the easting.. 245
3. Take the south edge of the grid square in
   which the point lies and read the large figures
   opposite this line on the east or west margin........... 64
   Estimate tenths from the grid line to the
   point (distance n)....................................... 8
   The resulting three figure number is the northing....... 648
4. The full 100 metre reference is given by
   writing first the letters, followed by the
   easting and then by the northing.................. NN 245648

---

square are further broken down into 100 by 100, 1km squares; it's these that are found on your map. By using the correct grid letters you can distinguish between our two grid squares in Figure 4.3. So where on your map do you find which grid letters your map is within?

Figure 4.5 is taken from the key of an Explorer map. The small square labelled NN denotes which part of the country the map covers; in this case Scotland. The letters are also repeated in the corner squares of every map and also either side of the 00 line (Figure 4.6). It's not always necessary to give grid letters but if you want complete accuracy and to avoid all doubt then give the letters as well.

*4.5 The National Grid Reference System explained on an Explorer map*

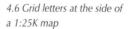

*4.6 Grid letters at the side of a 1:25K map*

Technological advances also mean that grid letters may one day come into their own. A grid reference is far more accurate than a postcode, for example. If only sat-navs in cars could understand these you could be taken to your exact destination and not just somewhere in the vicinity.

Let's leave the future behind, if that's metaphysically possible, and look at how we can become even more accurate with a grid reference.

In the example shown in Figure 4.1 we identified the church's grid reference as 05 33. This is all well and good, but imagine that instead of a church we were looking for a walker with a broken leg. If we gave a grid reference of 05 33 for the casualty, even if we gave the grid letters as well, this would actually describe an area of 1km², or 1000m by 1000m, or 1,000,000m². Try looking for a human being in a million square metres. To be able to give a more accurate location for our walker, the square needs to be divided further still.

### Six-Figure Grid References

Figure 4.7 shows a 1km square taken from the grid in Figure 4.1. Instead of the church, your unfortunate colleague (represented by the small square) is located at this spot. To identify this location more accurately, a six-figure grid reference is needed. To do this, I have subdivided the square into a hundred smaller squares by drawing 10 vertical and 10 horizontal lines equally spaced from one another. (On a 1:25,000 map this would be every 4mm, which represents 100 metres on the ground.) So the

*4.7 Reading a six-figure grid reference*

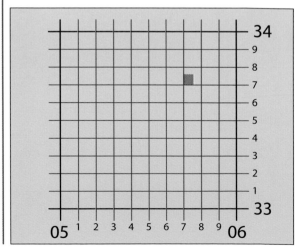

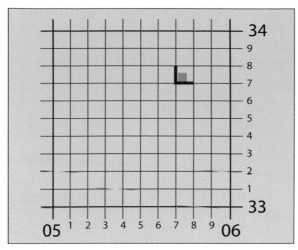

*4.8 Drawing an 'L' around the object will reveal the grid reference*

vertical line 05 becomes 050, then 051, 052 going up to the far-right line, which is 060. Similarly, the horizontal lines are numbered from 0 to 9 from the bottom up, so here the numbers of the lines become 330, 31 and so on to 340. Having done that, the reading of the grid reference is done in the same manner as before. This gives us a six-figure grid reference for the walker of 057 337. Note that the first two digits of each half are the same as before (05 and 33). By using six-figure grid references we have effectively divided the square down into 100 by 100m squares. Ten thousand square metres is easier to search than one million!

Another way of identifying the grid reference is to draw a capital L round the feature, along the nearest grid lines. Figure 4.8 shows this technique applied to Figure 4.7.

The advantage of drawing the 'L' is that it not only ensures you read the lower of the two possible vertical and horizontal grid lines but that, by drawing the 'L' from the top left corner to the bottom right corner, it ensures you read the vertical grid line number first and the horizontal second. On Figure 4.8, the vertical arm of the L lies on the 057 grid line, and the horizontal line on the 337 line; hence the six-figure grid reference of 057 337. (This technique will obviously work for a four-figure grid reference – you'd just draw the 'L' along the major grid lines that are on the map.)

It's now worth practising a few grid references. The key of an OS map shows an example worked out for you using a location on that map. Try it for yourself and then chose other points and work out the references for those.

## USING A ROMER

Let's think practically for a while. You're on the hill and working out a six-figure grid reference. You're not going to get out your ruler and pencil to sub-divide a grid square are you? Fortunately, there are two other ways of working out a grid reference. The first is to use your eye to estimate how many tenths across and up the square your desired location is. Even by eye, you can, with practice, become fairly accurate.

**1:25,000 Romer**

**1:50,000 Romer**

*4.9 Romers for 1:25,000 and 1:50,000 maps*

The second is to use a Romer – a scale which divides the grid box up for you. Figure 4.9 illustrates a 1:25,000 and a 1:50,000 Romer. You can buy these and some compasses have them printed onto their base plates. It is, however, very easy to make one: mark points from the top right-hand corner at either 2mm intervals for a 1:50,000 Romer, or 4mm for a 1:25,000 Romer (Figure 4.10)

To use your handcrafted piece of technology, place the corner of the Romer onto the object you wish to locate. Once again, walk along the corridor before climbing the stairs and read the figure on the Romer against the (left-hand) vertical grid line first followed by the Romer figure next to the (lower) horizontal line, as illustrated in Figure 4.11.

The six-figure reference is confirmed as 057 337. (**Note** If your position is between two numbers, always take the lower of the two possible numbers for your grid reference.)

*4.10 Some compasses (L) have Romers printed on their base plate but you can also make your own (R)*

If you look again at Figure 4.11, you'll see the grid lines lie between the Romer's vertical and horizontal 7 and 8 numbers. This means that we can increase the level of

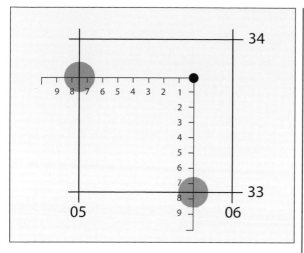

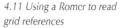

*4.11 Using a Romer to read grid references*

accuracy from a six-figure reference to an eight-figure one. The more accurate reference on the above diagram would be 0575 3375. (The fourth and eighth figures are '5' as the line is dissected midway between the 7 and 8 figures.)

Figure 4.12 shows a Romer in action on a printed map. The grid reference for the top of Swinside is 1760 2430. Using an eight-figure reference means that the level of accuracy is taken down to a 10 by 10m² level. Take care though: if you were to give an eight-figure reference to a mountain rescue team as the location of your unfortunate chum, then you need to be pretty certain you are at that location.

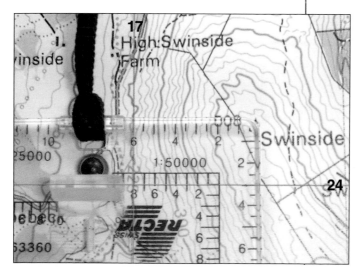

*4.12 With its corner at the top of Swinside, the Romer shows that the summit is 60 units east of the vertical gridline (17) and 30 units north of the horizontal gridline (24) so the full grid ref is 1760 2430 – the rounded corner makes accuracy harder*

53

If you don't want to buy (or make) a separate Romer and your compass doesn't have one, you can use the ruler on the side of your compass. On a 1:25,000 map the grid squares are 4cm apart so the extra vertical and horizontal subdivisions occur every 4mm (2mm on a 1:50,000 map). Count the number of 4mm sections (or count the total number of millimetres and divide by 4) across from the first vertical line and then the number of 4mm sections up from the horizontal line to get your accurate grid reference. Diagram 4.13 shows this in action. The first half of the grid reference for the stream, junction A is 284.

## SETTING THE MAP

*4.13 Use the millimetre scale on your compass to read grid references if you don't have a Romer.*

Here is a question for you, dear reader: how many times have you started a walk... in the wrong direction? Before you splutter out 'Never, you cheeky young rascal', I'll hold my hand up and confess to making this mistake on

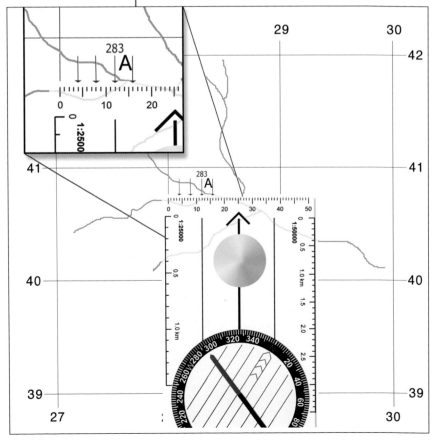

a couple of occasions. It's easily done of course. You're all relaxed and jocular and the last thing anybody does is to actually check the map! So, how can you prevent the red-dening of cheeks? By setting the map.

Turn the map so the linear feature on the map is parallel to the linear feature on the ground. This is shown here by the red dashed line on the map which is parallel to the dashed line going through the landscape.

Setting a map means you turn the map so that a feature on the ground corresponds with its land-scape in exactly the same way that it does on the map. So, for instance, a land-mark appears, say, on your right-hand side while you are walking along a path. If your map is set correctly the feature will also be shown on the right of the path on the map. Figure 4.14 shows just this.

4.14 Setting a map using linear features

There are two ways to set the map. First, use a long linear feature, like a path or road, and turn the map so that the line of the feature on the map coincides with the way it runs on the ground. The second, and slightly more accu-rate, way is to take out your compass and line the vertical grid lines with the red end of the needle. Even though I don't discuss using a compass in detail until Chapter 7, it is appropriate to mention here that the red end points north. By pointing the red end of the needle along the ver-tical grid lines and towards the northern edge of the map, you are setting the map. This is shown in Figure 4.15.

Once you've set the map, you will have to keep turn-ing it as your route changes direction. You'll find this a bit awkward to start with but after a while you'll be doing it automatically. Setting the map will also help to avoid making mistakes with your map reading. Bear in mind, however, that there will be times when you'll be reading the map upside down or sideways on – nothing wrong with that as long as you know what you're doing!

*Using the compass to set a map*

4.15 A map set by lining the vertical grid lines up with the red end of the needle

Sometimes it's difficult keeping your place on your map while you're walking. Try thumbing – no, not hitching to the nearest pub. Thumbing in this context means placing your thumb on your location on the map. Alternatively, try using an adhesive dot which you can move along as your location changes. This is especially effective on laminated maps (until they get too wet).

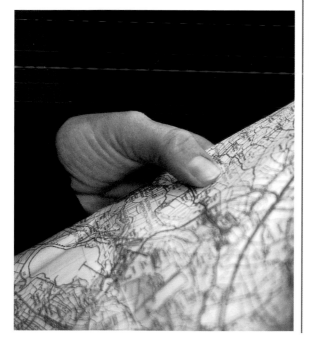

'Thumbing', or keeping your thumb on your location, will help you to keep your place on the map

57

*Dots on a map can also help you keep your place*

## BEWARE

As a lover of maps I find it difficult to draw on them and I go positively pale when I see how some folk treat them. A map is a great source of information but some people seem to go to great efforts to obscure that information by drawing over it. Out comes the blue felt tip and a great broad line is marked over the route – to help them keep their place on a walk, they claim. Disaster! Yes, you'll be able to see where your route is on a map, but your line may obscure some vital piece of information that makes the difference between getting lost and that pile of chips and pint of tea at the end of the walk!

## Key Points

- The national grid means every place in the UK has its own unique grid reference.
- The more numbers in your grid reference, the more accurate it is.
- Romers, or the scale on the side of a compass, can help to work out accurate grid references.
- Setting a map to the land helps avoid silly mistakes.
- Use adhesive dots, or your thumb, to help keep your place on a map.

# CHAPTER FIVE

# UNDERSTANDING CONTOURS

## IN THIS CHAPTER YOU'LL LEARN ABOUT

- contours
- concave, convex and straight slopes
- contour spacing
- how to read the shape of the landscape from contour lines

# Chapter 5

At some time or other a walker will come across a hill! Some people don't like going up, some don't like going down and some just hate them entirely. However, hills are there and being able to spot them on the map is an important skill to acquire; to do this it is necessary to be able to read contours.

Put simply, a contour is a line joining points of equal height. One way of considering this is to think of an island (Figure 5.1). At low tide the sea is at Level 1. An hour later the tide has risen 1m to Level 2, after another hour the sea has risen a further 1m to Level 3 and so on. Leaving aside the complexity of tidal variation, the tide lines are what contours are – lines joining places of equal height.

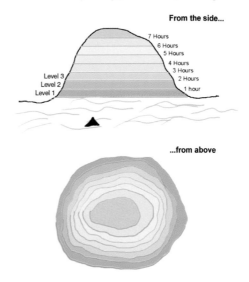

**From the side...**

7 Hours
6 Hours
5 Hours
4 Hours
3 Hours
2 Hours
1 hour

Level 3
Level 2
Level 1

**...from above**

*5.1 An island with successive sea levels and how it might look from above as 'contours'*

The contour interval varies depending on both the scale of map and the version of map you are using. Taking OS maps first: on 1:50,000 maps the interval is 10m; on upland 1:25,000 maps the interval is also 10m; but on lowland 1:25,000s they are spaced at 5m intervals. Harvey's maps use 10 or 15m contours. There is one map from Ireland that uses both 5 and 10m on the same hill! Confused? They certainly must have been.

But, I have also been confused from time to time, having misread contours, assuming a slope is gentler than

*Terraced hillsides in Nepal follow the land's natural contours*

it turns out to be and, on one notable occasion, believing the route was downhill, when in reality it was up! (I wasn't popular!) The lesson? Check on the map what the contour interval is and in what direction the slopes are heading.

Look at Figure 5.2. The contours are shown by the continuous brown lines. You'll note that every fifth line is darker and slightly thicker than the others. On this extract, from a Harvey map, the height difference between each darker line is 75m. Looking at these particular lines helps when working out how far you've got to climb or descend. It goes without saying that contours are not visible on the ground, however sometimes the contrary is true too, and a land feature that you think should be represented by a change in contours isn't shown on the map. For example, you may be navigating across a hillside and come to a depression in the ground. You look closely at the map but can't see a reference to it. Rather than thinking you're in the wrong place it may be that the depression is smaller than the map's contour interval

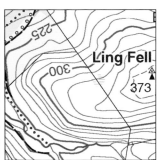

*5.2 What do these squiggly brown lines mean?*

and falls between two successive contours. It could also mean the map makers left it off by mistake – they are human after all.

It is also easy to look at the fifth thicker contour and assume there is some significant feature here. Every year I run a contour-only course, where we go onto Kinder Scout with a map with just the contour and grid lines on. When faced with nowt but the squiggly brown things it's easy to latch on to some hope that the thicker ones are more significant than the thinner ones. This just isn't the case.

## INTERPRETING CONTOURS

It is important to start with the basic principles of contours – being able to read contours is an incredibly powerful weapon in your navigational armoury. Take a look at Figure 5.3. The straight section of the diagram (part A) shows the contour lines equally spaced. If you think this

*5.3 Straight, concave and convex slopes and how they may appear on a map*

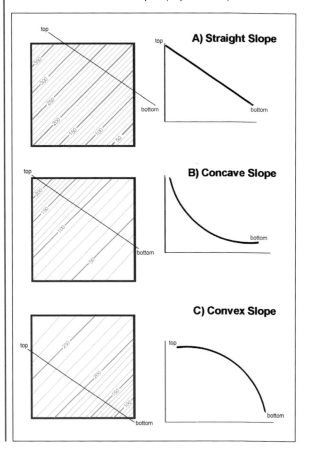

5.4 In reality slopes are never as simple as Figure 5.3 might suggest A=straight, B=concave, C=convex

through, it means that as you climb you walk the same distance between each successive contour. The concave slope (part B) has contours lines that are wider apart at the foot of the slope but which get closer together towards the top. The convex happens in reverse: the contours start closer together and then gradually get further apart as you get to the top. These slopes can be quite misleading, as you never see the summit until you get to the top. (I call convex slopes Julie Andrews Slopes. If you remember the film there was the cameraman struggling up to the summit of this convex hill and suddenly he was engulfed in be-curtained children and singing nuns. He never saw her coming… poor bloke!)

That all seems simple enough but in reality it is rarely so, and you're more likely to get composite slopes made up of two or more of the above. However, having an appreciation of the basic types and being able to spot from the map what a slope is likely to look like will help in your quest for navigational perfection.

## THE CLOSENESS OF CONTOURS

The closeness of contours is something you also should be aware of. As shown in Figure 5.3, the closer they are, the steeper the ground. If you know you don't like steep slopes then look for paths that go up wider-spaced contours or paths that cross the contours at an angle. An area of tightly packed contours means steep ground and pain.

Take a look at Figure 5.5a. Have you noticed how the numbers have been written on the contour lines? Contour numbers are always written looking up the hill regardless of whether the numbers appear upside down or sideways when holding the map with the north at the top. This is again a useful way of determining slope direction and orientation.

*5.5a Looking carefully at the contours now will make it easier on the hill*

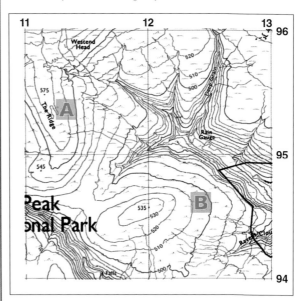

*5.5b On the ground the spot height is difficult to locate accurately*

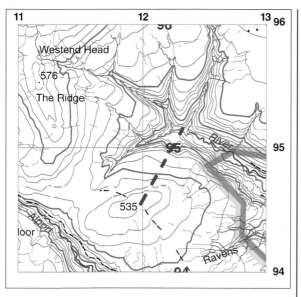

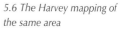

5.6 The Harvey mapping of the same area

## ADVANCED CONTOUR READING

But there is more we can read from contours. Figure 5.5a shows a lovely sloping area with lots of contours to get your teeth into. Look first at the 535 spot height, grid reference 120 945. (It is labelled in brown because the height has been determined by aerial survey and not a ground survey.) This is a broad-topped hill with gentle slopes which becomes slightly steeper to the north (the contours are closer here). The fact that the spot height is 5m higher than the nearest contour line will imply that the hill isn't flat-topped but continues to rise gently to the top. (Spot heights are like contours and are not visible on the ground (see Figure 5.5.b) – so you'll not be bumping into brown spots!)

There are a number of streams running off the hill. But look to the east of the hill to see the slight nicks in the 510 and 500m contour lines (B); these would imply that there is a channel running down that way too. The fact that there isn't a stream marked implies that there may be a seasonal channel or one grassed over which wasn't visible when the map was drawn. (The Harvey map of this area (Figure 5.6) shows a different pattern of streams and illustrates how the OS and Harvey mapping shows water features differently.)

Moving north-west to The Ridge (see Figure 5.5a), you can see a slight indentation on the slope implying something has carved out the gap between the two small spurs

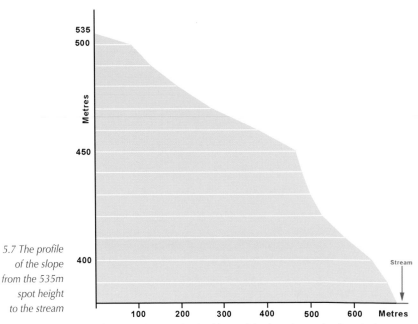

5.7 The profile
of the slope
from the 535m
spot height
to the stream

Of course, the horizontal scale of this graph has been shortened so that it fits the page.
(The slope isn't really this steep!)

of land (A). Again, the Harvey map shows this area differently, although neither one is right or wrong. Looking at Figure 5.6 you will see a dashed contour line, which they call an auxiliary line around the 576 spot height. This is an intermediate contour at a 5m interval drawn in to help with discerning the shape of the ground. It's not essential, but useful nevertheless.

Imagine you were walking from the 535m summit to the kink in the river near the bottom of the valley (grid reference 123 951, as shown by the red dashed line in Figure 5.6). Picture in your mind what you'll be walking over. You'll start at the hilltop, and descend reasonably gently from the spot height to the first contour. The gap between the first and second contour is quite small implying a short steep section, then between the second and fourth contours it's gentler and between the fourth and sixth even gentler. After this 60m descent from the top (six contour lines), the slope steepens suddenly and you descend 40m in height in a short horizontal distance (less than 100m). The slope then eases and the next 20m drop takes you 150 horizontal metres to the stream. Figure 5.7 shows this in profile.

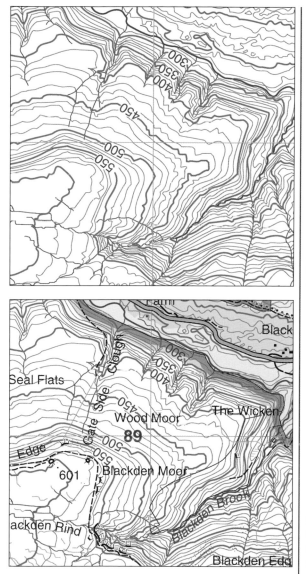

5.8 Although you won't have the luxury of a stripped-down map like this...

5.9 ... try to disregard the other features and concentrate only on the contours

## ANTICIPATION AND AWARENESS

Being able to anticipate what you're about to walk over is useful, helping you to avoid silly mistakes. Look carefully at the map and imagine what the terrain will do. If it differs from reality, alarm bells should start ringing and a check back to the map should reveal your error – are you in the wrong place on the map or have you got yourself somewhere on the ground that you weren't intending to go?

*Winter sun in the Peak District – the paths may be invisible but the walls and contours of the hills provide sound navigation pointers*

Looking at the lie of the ground between the 535m hilltop and The Ridge in Figure 5.6, can you see its shape? You'll descend gently and then begin to climb to an ever-narrowing ridge of land.

Being able to 'see' landforms from contours alone is an incredibly powerful skill and perhaps one of the most difficult challenges you'll face when learning to navigate.

Figure 5.8 shows a version of the Harvey map showing just contours and grid lines. While you won't have the 'luxury' of such a map, if you can see through the other features to the contours beneath your naviagtion will be better for it.

## HOW DEEP IS THE VALLEY?

You'll recall that different maps have different contour intervals. Figure 5.10 shows two map extracts taken from maps with these two different contour intervals. They both show a valley side (A to B). Figure 5.10a looks like a very deep valley and Figure 5.10b in comparison looks far shallower.

In reality, the slope from A to B in Figure 5.10a (Kirk Dale) climbs around 50m, whereas from Cranberry Clough to Little Moor Top (A to B) down to the stream in Figure 5.10b climbs 90m! The different contour interval can make a shallower valley look far worse than it really is. If you're moving onto a new map check what the contour interval is! It will tell you in the key.

As ever practice is the only way forward. When you go to a new location, sit on top of a hill, spread out your map and try to match the landscape below you with the way it's represented on the map. Another excellent way of helping yourself to get to grips with contours is to use the excellent digital mapping programmes available for computers. Most of these have a function which will show the 2D map in 3 dimensions. (Figures 5.11a and b) Spending time looking at the contours on a 2D map and deciding on the shape of the ground in 3D is a fabulous way of getting to grips with contours – as ever the more time you

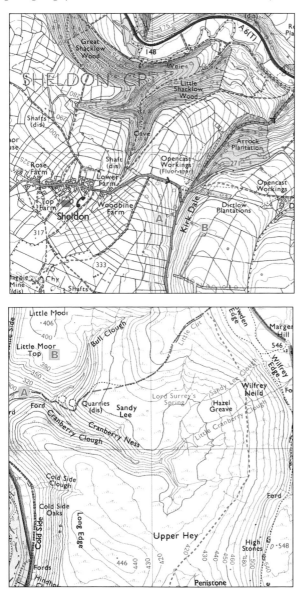

5.10a Looking at the contour interval is advisable. The slope A to B on this map is gentler than...

5.10b ...this slope A to B

*5.11a Digital mapping software enables you to study a map in 2D...*

*5.11b ...and then see what it looks like in 3D*

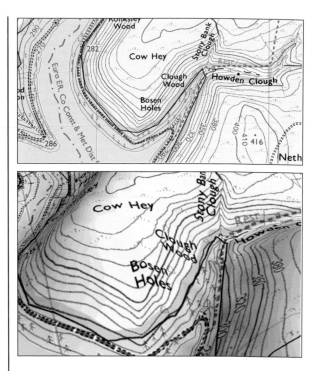

spend looking at maps the more familiar you'll become with all aspects of them.

Contours aren't easy to get you head around, hence devoting a whole chapter to the subject. Fully understanding them will take time and, as ever, practice. Once you've mastered them, they'll reward your perseverance many times over. It's worth spending time over them.

## Key Points

- Contours are lines joining points of equal height.
- Contour intervals vary depending on the scale and make of map you're using. Check the scale of the map that you are using.
- Every fifth contour is drawn in heavier ink.
- The closer the contours are spaced, the steeper the slope.
- Reading the shape of the ground from map contours is an important skill to acquire.

# CHAPTER SIX

# PLANNING YOUR WALKS

**IN THIS CHAPTER YOU'LL LEARN ABOUT**

- planning walks
- leader's responsibilities
- how terrain, weather and group members can affect your plans
- route cards
- Naismith's Rule
- safety on walks

# Chapter 6

*We keep walking but we never get there.*

from the film 'Himalaya' by Eric Valli

**B**y now you're probably chomping at the bit and wanting to get out there and put some of your map skills to work. Relax, you're almost there. There's just the small matter of planning to consider.

However, let's first consider what you want from a walk. There are probably as many reasons why people walk as there are people walking! Some people want to clock up as many miles as possible, some want a pleasant after-dinner stroll and others want a challenging hike followed by a good pint and a meal. Only you know why you walk and what you want to get out of your day, and this should be at the forefront of your mind while you plan a walk. If you want a gentle afternoon stroll don't plan a 20-mile walk!

## WALK LEADER'S RESPONSIBILITY

If you are planning a walk for friends or your local rambling group, you need to be aware that as soon as you take on some form of responsibility, whether formal or informal, you need to consider the others in your group. You may be hyper-fit but there may be others in your group who aren't. Plan a walk that the weakest member can do. After all, the walk is for them and not for you. If

*So, off we went into the Pyrenean mist*

*Mam Tor may look innocent – whatever the conditions attention is always needed*

you want to do something more macho, walk with different people.

Having received an invitation from a friend who was coming over to the Peak District for a walk I decided it would be fun to join them and walk without any responsibility (on most of the walks I do, I am the guide). So, I met up with them and we walked up to Mam Tor, which is one of the few peaks in the Peak District. We started to ascend the stone steps to the summit only to be met by one of the strongest winds I've had the pleasure of encountering. Our 'leader' and two others cut into the wind with little difficulty and disappeared into the distance. Being not insubstantially built, I also managed reasonably well. However, six of the group were lightweight and were in danger of being blown off the edge. Having got to the top I spent about 15 minutes helping the strugglers. We sat on the top exhausted, cold and more than a little nervous about the conditions. (We'd lost two hats to the wind.) It didn't take much to persuade the group to abandon the hill in favour of a less windy option.

In fact, I quite enjoyed the experience but the other six weren't happy. The lesson for the day? On seeing the conditions our leader should have turned the group around. He might have been able to cope, but more than half of his group couldn't: he should have spotted this and acted accordingly. As a walk leader take a lesson from Buddhism: shed your ego and think of the others first.

## BEFORE YOU GO

Whether you are walking alone, with friends or as a group leader, there are a number of aspects of the day to consider in advance.

### Weather

English weather is generally unstable and varies in severity. A pleasant walk you did in August may be a very different prospect in January (and vice versa!). However, British weather forecasts are getting better and it may be possible when planning your walk to get a fair picture of the conditions you'll be walking in. There are numerous websites that give general weather forecasts but remember that they aren't aimed at hill or mountain goers. The Mountain Weather Information Service (www.mwis.org. uk) has detailed forecasts available for most of Scotland, the Lake District, The Pennines and the Peak District and Snowdonia.

If the purpose of your walk is to walk in foul conditions, testing both your waterproof gear and navigational skills (and there's nothing wrong with this as an aim), then a high moorland walk as a cold front is passing over may be just what you want. Most of us prefer walking in better conditions, and picking a sheltered route during such a storm is probably wise.

Once you've planned a walk, however, conditions on the day may mean you have to change, or abandon, your plans. A good leader is a flexible one.

### Terrain and Route

The terrain is another important consideration. If you normally do 15 miles a day in East Anglia, a walking trip to the Lakes may require a slight readjustment in terms of distance! There is a formula, Naismith's Rule, that will be introduced below that will help you to work out how far you are likely to walk in a day.

What about refreshment points and transport arrangements? If you have the transport available a linear walk can often be more fulfilling than a circular walk. With the latter, it is sometimes inevitable that you'll have to retrace

*Jeans, duffle coat and handbag aren't generally suitable attire for a walk in the mist in winter*

your steps and, if the weather is poor or you are leading others, this could mean the walk ends on a downer. You want your companions to finish a walk still enjoying it!

## Points of Interest

Generally speaking, unless you are one of those mystifying people who likes to clock up over 20 miles in a day, you will probably want to spend a little time looking at something of interest. When planning a walk, I always try to include good views, high points, something of historical interest and so on. Why? First, because they make a walk more interesting, and second, they provide a good excuse to sit down, whip out the flask and have a rest.

So how do you find out about these good stopping points? Obviously, if you know the area you intend to walk in then you probably won't need to think about it. If you are walking in a new area, then study a guidebook, ask a local, visit an information centre, surf the internet or study the map. You'd research an area well before a holiday, so why not for a day's walk?

I remember accompanying an organised group walk in an area new to me, hoping to learn more about it. Sadly, the group leader spent all his time at the front of the group, forcing the pace and we never stopped at points that interested the rest of the group. In fact we only stopped when the 'tail-end Charlie' got lost! How that walk would have been enhanced if we'd learnt something about the area.

## Using a Guidebook

One of the benefits of learning to navigate mentioned at the beginning of this manual was the ability to leave your guidebooks behind. Now I'm telling you to study them! The point is that guidebooks have their place, but not as big a place as many walkers give them. By all means, use them to plan your day and pick out an interesting walk, but why not adapt it to suit your needs?

Use your map to find interesting areas too. I discovered my favourite limestone dale in the Peak District that way. It was in an area traditionally dismissed as it was close to a large quarry. However, the map showed a dale that ended at the quarry. A walk down there revealed a delightful place, full of orchids, cowslips and other interesting flora and, because of its location, not many people walk there either. A sheer delight and one whose location I'm keeping secret. You'll have to discover it for yourself!

*Use guides, but not slavishly*

## How Far?

Let's move on. You've found an area and know what points of interest you want to visit. Next it is important to turn your attention to the walk itself. Only you know how far you want to walk: but how do you translate that onto the map? There are two ways, one of which is more accurate than the other.

The first uses string; it's a wonderful invention and one underused by most walkers. Mark a piece of thin parcel-string with felt-tip pen every 4cm (the equivalent of 1km on a 1:25,000 map). Placing one end on the starting point, lay it along the intended route, ensuring it finishes at a suitable end-point at the required distance! What is suitable will vary, but it may have to be accessible for transport or be at a public loo and so on. This highly technical piece of string works well and has the incentive of being cheap!

*Not everything in life needs to be hi-tech: a pedometer, map wheel and string!*

(I once met a woman on a map and compass course I was tutoring who apologised that her mother wasn't with her, being unwell. She asked if she could see my piece of string as her mother had specifically asked her to look at it! What could a kind-hearted soul do but make a present of it to her mother – I just hope it made her better!)

The other method involves a pair of tools I'd rather not donate. Holding your index and middle fingers 4cm apart, carefully estimate how far the intended walk is going to be, adjusting the route if it's too much or too little. Admittedly it's not very scientific but it isn't too inaccurate either.

Some people use map wheels to measure map distances, backing them up by using pedometers on the hill. Pedometers, those little instruments hung from the belt that are supposed to tell you how far you've walked, work by 'counting' the wearer's strides (at a length previously set) and translating this into distance. However, they are invariably inaccurate: most of us take different stride lengths according to the terrain and underfoot conditions.

## ROUTE CARDS

Planning a walk is all very well, but remembering the decisions you made the previous evening may be difficult when you're out in gale-force winds with freezing rain dripping down your neck. The best way of remembering them is to write them down – enter the route card. Route cards are important for summarising your planned walk: time, distance and height climbed are all detailed, alternative routes are noted and, importantly, it provides a means by which you can leave details of your walk with someone responsible in case you need help.

Figure 6.1 is a suggested format for a route card. (A copy of this route card is available on my website at www.silvanavigationschool.com.) Taking each column in turn, let's consider what information is need. The first two columns, 'from' and 'to', require you to identify the points you're navigating from and to. Along with the name of the location or a description, insert a six-figure grid reference too. This information is important for you to be able to find the spot on the map during your walk. Just a grid reference would do, but this would add to the work you would have to do while on the hill – you'd have to locate the gridline numbers and go through the rigmarole of constructing the grid reference again; instead, having the name or description can help you

# ROUTECARD

Date:

Group Members:

Home contact details:

| From (Grid Ref and Name) | To (Grid Ref and Name) | Magnetic Bearing | Height Climbed (m) | Distance (km) | Time Taken (mins) | Notes |
|---|---|---|---|---|---|---|
| | | | | | | |
| | | | | | | |
| | | | | | | |
| | | | | | | |
| | | | | | | |
| | | | | | | |
| | | | | | | |
| | | | | | | |
| | | | | | | |

Alternative Route(s):

Accommodation:

Magnetic Variation for year _____ is _____ °W or E

6.1 A good route card can save a lot of bother on the hill

relocate the point quickly. This information is also useful if your route card is being used by others to find you (more of this later).

## Dividing up Your Walk

There is no hard and fast rule of how many sections you should break your walk into. If you are navigating on a compass bearing, too long a length (say over 1km) may cause you to make errors, as you'll discover later on in the book. However, if you're on an obvious footpath you can get away with a longer section. Generally speaking, when planning a day's walk of 10 to 12 miles it is likely that you'll use most of the lines of this illustrated route card. Too few sections, or legs, would mean that you are not giving yourself enough help on the hill; too many and you are over complicating the walk. Remember, the whole purpose of going walking is to enjoy yourself. If you spend all your time poring over a route card, this enjoyment goes out of the window!

Furthermore, when you're out walking a leg of a route card, you can subdivide the route still further by using a technique called 'ticking off'.

## Ticking Off

Before you start a leg of a journey, identify particular features along the route, such as a kink in the footpath, the edge of a wood, a particular outcrop of rock or other characteristics of the land. As you pass them, mentally tick them off – this is known as 'ticking off' points. Again, this may seem daunting at first but you'll find it becomes automatic as your skills develop (see Figure 6.2).

## Magnetic Bearing

The next column, labelled 'magnetic bearing', will mean more when you have read Chapter 7, but suffice to say that this is the angle you dial into your compass to set you in the right direction. However, you may not need a bearing if your walk is entirely along footpaths – you'll be in a better position to decide this once you've mastered the compass in Chapter 7.

While we're on the subject of the magnetic variation, as you'll soon discover it changes in value over time. Make a note of the date and variation for when you write the route card, so that when you want to walk the route again, you know by how much you'll have to alter the magnetic bearings.

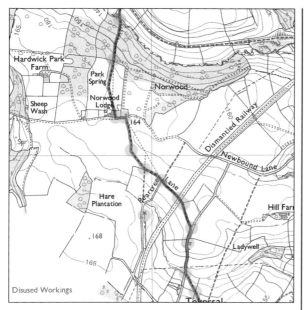

6.2 Features,
such as those highlighted
along the route on this
map, can be used to
'tick off' your progress

## Height Climbed

You'll be aware that it takes longer to walk a given distance up a hill than on the flat, and so considering the amount of climbing on the route will help determine the time it takes you to do the walk. The 'height climbed' column records the height climbed on each leg. Generally speaking downhill walking speed isn't very different from that on the flat. However, if you're very slow coming downhill, which is particularly likely if the slope is very steep, by all means amend this column by adding the height descended.

To fill in the 'height climbed' section count the number of contours the leg crosses and, noting the contour interval from the map's key, insert the appropriate figure into the column.

## Distance

Here you need to whip out your string and measure how long each particular leg is. Do bear in mind you are measuring the distance the 'crow flies'. If there are lots of ups and downs, then you will walk further than this (although adding in the height climbed compensates for this).

## Time

To calculate the 'time taken' column, Naismith's Rule should be used. The Victorian Scotsman Naismith was one of those fine gentlemen who spent his leisured existence doing Useful Things for the good of society! Naismith strode the hills, stopwatch and notebook in hand, religiously recording how long it took him to get to specific points and then how long to get back! His life's work was not in vain because we now have a rule named after him. His original imperial rule is now used in the metric form.

## Time Taken = 4km/hr + 1 minute for every 10m climbed

When working out time taken for lengths less than 1km, rather than assuming a walking speed of 1km in 15 minutes it is easier to use 16 minutes. Why? For the plain and simple reason that dividing into 16 is easier than dividing into 15!

**Our walk is 3.4km long and climbs 240m – how long would Naithsmith say it takes?**

If it takes 1hr to walk 4km, then it takes 15 minutes to walk 1km. It will therefore take 45 minutes for 3km and 400m will take approximately 6 minutes.

If it takes 1 minute to climb 10m, it must take 24 minutes to climb 240m.

**Therefore, Time Taken = 45 + 6 + 24 = 75 minutes**

(Bear in mind what was mentioned above while discussing height. If you're in the dodgy-knees brigade perhaps apply the same equation to descent as to climbing, and add an extra minute for every 10m you go down.)

Ok, if Naismith's Rule lived up to its name we wouldn't have room for such approximations. Everyone walks at different speeds, so the assumption that wee Naismith makes about walking at 4km an hour is wrong. Correct! However, 4km an hour is a good guide to the approximate speed of a group over a day. In truth, we all walk at different speeds so you should adapt Naismith's Rule accordingly. Start by assuming you walk at 4km an hour but adjust it to suit your situation and experience.

The formula is approximate for other reasons too. Different underfoot conditions will cause different walking speeds, as will the time of day; the tendency is to walk faster in the morning and slower in the afternoon. Use

Naismith's Rule as a guide to both the total walking time for a walk and also the approximate time for each leg, but don't take it too literally. (See Chapter 10 for more on Naismith.)

## Make Notes

The last column of the route card is the notes section. This is extremely useful, and much underused: it allows you to annotate the card to remind yourself about some of the decisions you made when you wrote the route out. It may be that one leg has a choice of footpaths; here you can remind yourself which one you decided on. The column could indicate where you intend to break for lunch, a useful piece of information if you are leading a walk and want to give your group an indication that you care about them! You can also use the notes section to write a short-hand description of the terrain you expect to encounter, which is another way to ensure you're on the right route. There are many more uses for the notes column, but in short, use it to help you on the walk.

## Other Information

So what else should the card contain? The date of the walk is vital. Imagine the situation. You leave the dateless route card at the information centre near the start of the walk. You forget to pick it up and during the day it falls under the desk. Two weeks later the cleaner comes across the paper on the floor, puts it on the desk and the information assistant at the end of the day realises you haven't picked it up and calls out the rescue team. You've been at home for two weeks! This also emphasises why home contact details are important. If the rescue team doesn't know where you live or are staying they can't check that you've got home safely either. The contact details may be the same as the 'accommodation' section; alternatively, if you are on holiday you would be wise to fill in both sections.

The final section is the 'alternative route' section. Other route card examples may call this part 'escape routes' or 'bad weather routes'. If you were planning a multi-day expedition and needed to consider the vagaries of the British weather you would have a ready-made alternative route for bad weather noted here. Apart from that, this has little use for day walkers.

The title 'escape route' is also a little limiting. Some believe you need to plan escape routes off your planned

walk in case anything serious happens. Do you just choose the point where you are furthest from civilisation or do you note escape paths at regular intervals along the way? Whatever happens you can guarantee that an accident won't happen at any of your escape points! If you would like to use this section, it is thus probably best to refer to it as 'alternative routes'.

### Why use route cards?

Before moving on, it's worth discussing why route cards are important. I've dropped hints already but let's recap. First of all they are a good way of summarising a route to make your walk easier. Rather than poring over the map on the day, whip out the route card instead and there is your route, all neatly written out and easy to follow. Planning ahead also means you are more likely to spot alternatives that may be more interesting than the obvious. It may also be late in the day and cold and your companions are breathing down your neck wanting a quick navigational decision from you on the hill. These conditions aren't conducive to creativity – a pre-planned route card is your best solution.

The second reason I've hinted at too: safety. Whenever I lead a party out on a walk, I leave a route card with someone responsible, be it a colleague, an information centre, police station or whoever I can rely on to do the right thing if I don't return. It may sound a bit dramatic I suppose, but giving a rescue team an idea of where you are walking is a great help. Having a route pre-planned doesn't mean you have to stick to it religiously, as people who have walked with me will well understand – no rescue team would expect you to anyway – but at least they have a rough idea of where you are.

The Peak District's seven mountain rescue teams were called out one Christmas to look for a man who had collapsed on the hill. He'd met up with another walker during the day and they'd decided to walk together. The trouble came once the guy had collapsed and his new companion didn't know where they were. The companion hurried off the hill and called mountain rescue. The teams had to search a good proportion of Bleaklow, as no one was certain where the collapsed man was and what route his companion had taken off the hill.

Compare that with a search in thick mist for a group of Duke of Edinburgh's Award students. One lad had badly broken his leg but once the call was made, despite the fact there was a thick mist on Kinder, he was found quickly. Why? As the group had prepared and handed a route card to someone responsible, the rescue team could walk the route both ways until reaching them. An efficient rescue, and all because there was a route card.

A word of warning though. If you leave a route card with someone, you need to pick it up again when you finish your walk. Give them a phone call or, preferably, collect it personally and bin it yourself.

There is another less important reason for completing a route card that could be interesting or useful in the long run. If you keep every route card you produce and file them, you have a terrific record of where you have walked. I have my routes stored on computer, and when I fill in a card, not only do I have a permanent record but the program also works Naismith's Rule out for me too. Oh the power of technology! And talking of technology, there are now some computer programs which combine digital maps with route planning software. Turn to Chapter 14 to find out more.

Now some of you may be wondering at this stage why there is such a strong emphasis on the route card. Surely not all walks need one? It all depends on where you intend walking. A stroll round the lanes of Surrey perhaps wouldn't require elaborate safety plans but things would be different in Scotland or the Lake District. If in doubt, prepare a route card.

When you start to prepare them, you will doubtless discover what I did at first. It was on a Mountain

| ROUTECARD | Dark Peak Explorer OL1 Date: 20th August 2003 | Group Members: Alan Jones, Tom and Jane Smith | | | | Home contact details: Alan Jones, 1 A Street, Town, County. 01387 111111 |
|---|---|---|---|---|---|---|
| From (Grid Ref and Name) | To (Grid Ref and Name) | Magnetic Bearing | Height Climbed (m) | Distance (km) | Time Taken (mins) | Notes |
| Hayfield 036 872 | Footpath Start 040 868 | | | 0.5 | 8 | Follow the road |
| Footpath Start 040 868 | Access point Snake Path 044 880 | | 110 | 1.5 | 34 | Path climbs gently across fields |
| Access point Snake Path 044 880 | Path Junctions 050 883 | 67 | 20 | 0.5 | 10 | |
| Path Junctions 050 883 | Wall Junctions 059 887 | | | 1.5 | 23 | Follow path downhill to reservoir side walk round to wall junction |
| Wall Junctions 059 887 | Path Junctions 063 902 | 22 | 220 | 1.5 | 45 | Follow path beside the stream |
| Path Junctions 063 902 | Access point Nr Pub 032 902 | 275 | 40 | 3 | 49 | Follow path via Mill & Burnt Hill or take bearing if poor visibility |
| Access point Nr Pub 032 902 | Matleymoor Farm 024 895 | | | 1.5 | 23 | Take road for 400m turn left & follow path downhill to Farm |
| Matleymoor Farm 024 895 | Path Junctions 025 889 | | 20 | 0.65 | 12 | Take the Bridleway |
| Path Junctions 025 889 | Minor Road 032 873 | | | 1.9 | 29 | Take 2nd path (135°) once on track stick on it until you reach the road |
| Minor Road 032 873 | Hayfield 036 869 | | | 0.6 | 9 | Follow the minor road (turn left) |
| | | | | 13.15 Km | 242 minutes 4hrs 2 minutes | |

Alternative Route(s):

Accommodation: Castleton Youth Hostel

Magnetic Variation for year _____ is _____ °W or E

6.3 An example of a filled-in route card

Leadership training course. We took six hours to plan a four-hour walk! There were mitigating circumstances, honest. A few bottles of wine did get in the way and the idea was to contrive a route between A and B so that the two-hour direct walk would actually take four. That's my excuse and I'm sticking to it, but the more you use route cards the faster you'll be able to produce them. I take around five minutes per card now!

Figure 6.3 is a sample route card illustrating what your completed one might look like. This route was chosen for a variety of reasons. First of all it takes in an area of open moorland, which if time permits could allow opportunities to explore further. It's also a historically significant area: the walk up William Clough is the route the famous Mass Trespassers took in 1932, which led to the eventual establishment of English and Welsh National Parks and more recently the passing of the Countryside and Rights of Way Act (2000). There are fine views to be had from Mill Hill and the walk ends on lower ground passing through farmland before returning to the start point.

Let's look in more detail at the route card. You'll notice that apart from the start and finish points there are no place names. There aren't many on the map either! The descriptions help to locate the points though. You may also be wondering why the 'magnetic bearing' column isn't fully filled in – as you will see in Chapter 7,

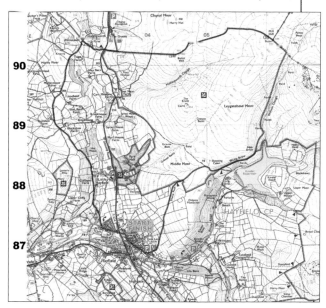

*Map illustrating the route as shown on the route card*

you don't have to use a compass all the time. If you are walking along a road or well-marked footpath a bearing is superfluous.

The 'height climbed' column has gaps in it too: why? The walk goes downhill at times and that, as you've learnt, doesn't generally affect the speed of walking. The 'Notes' column is there to remind you during your walk of why you made certain planning decisions when you wrote the card. For example, the sixth leg (from path junction to access point near pub) can be followed along the path on the ground. In poor visibility, however, following it may be difficult, so having the compass bearing written down just helps to make navigation easier on the day.

As you can see, completing a route card isn't rocket science. It is just a simple way of summarising your walking route, giving you all the details in an easy-to-read format. Get into the habit of filling in a route card and you'll find your navigation on the hill a far more pleasurable experience. You'll be able to spend your day enjoying the walk and not having to make up your route as you go along.

In Chapter 14 we discuss a couple of computer programs that allow you to plan routes on digital maps on screen. These have the potential to make route planning much easier and quicker. However, at this stage, planning a route by hand from a paper map is a good practice. I don't know about you, but I can read things more easily on paper than I can off a screen. Once you've mastered the basic skills manually, then you can look at more technical ways of doing things if you want to.

## Key Points

- Planning is the key to having a successful walk.
- A leader must consider a great deal: group ability, weather, terrain, points of interest, distance, and starting and finishing points.
- Route cards are a neat summary of a walk.
- Route cards cut down on vital decision-making while on the hill.
- Planning ahead speeds up the walk on the day.
- Pre-planning makes it more likely that you'll spot interesting alternatives.
- Route cards can be filed as a record of your walk.
- Route cards can be left with a responsible person in case of problems.

# INTRODUCING THE COMPASS

## IN THIS CHAPTER YOU'LL LEARN ABOUT

- compasses: the minimum features yours should have

- the different types of compasses

- using compasses around the world

# *Chapter 7*

*I do not seek, I find.*

Pablo Picasso

The compass – what self-respecting walker doesn't have one? Glance around the bar of any popular walkers' haunt and I suspect you'll see a few dangling around necks or off map cases. They have become the badge of honour, something that no walker should be without. Interestingly, however, ask most of those compass danglers how to use one and many won't be able to answer you. If they can, the explanation will be a touch garbled or even wrong. For such an elementary piece of kit invented by the Chinese thousands of years ago, which doesn't rely on batteries or microelectronics, many people seem to get terribly confused.

## THE BASICS

Elementary it is, too. There is nothing difficult about reading a compass. So before you persuade yourself otherwise, let's crack on and get the basics covered. Figure 7.1 is an

*7.1 A beginner's compass: yours should have these features as a minimum*

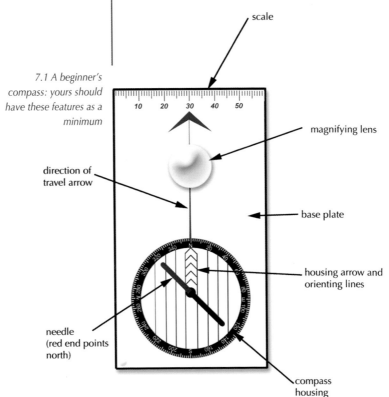

scale

magnifying lens

direction of travel arrow

base plate

housing arrow and orienting lines

needle (red end points north)

compass housing

example of a typical compass. It contains all you need from a compass without any of the extra twiddly bits that some compasses have.

The scale in this example is in millimetres, but it could be in centimetres or inches (if it's an old one), or even show distances according to different map scales as in Figure 7.2.

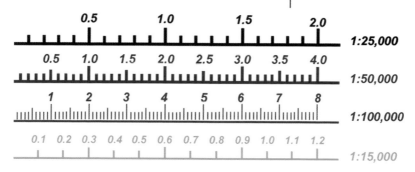

*7.2 Compass scales are sometimes drawn according to different map scales*

Compasses with scales like this (and some are interchangeable) can be useful in providing you with a quick indication of how far a particular leg is without having to do the mental maths to convert the map centimetres up to the walking metres or kilometres.

Some compasses have scales down the side too. Having scales on a compass is important; if yours doesn't then consider changing it. By the end of the chapter you'll have a better idea of what to buy.

Oh, how times change. When I wrote the first edition of this book in 2002, I put in the following glib sentences. 'Being a young thing, with full possession of all my faculties, I don't find I need a magnifying glass. However there will come a time, I'm sure, when I will have to rely on one.' Sad to say my eyes have now failed me and the magnifying lens is now the most used feature on my compass!

Some compasses have them and some don't. It isn't an essential part of a compass but a useful addition. Being able to magnify a small area of map, say as a footpath passes through a farmyard, can help to clarify where you should be walking. If you're buying a compass from scratch, then I'd suggest getting one with a magnifying glass; if you have a lensless one already, don't worry unless it needs replacing for other reasons. (You can, of course, buy a separate hand-held magnifying lens instead.)

Running through the lens from the edge of the compass housing is the direction of travel (DOT) arrow. This is

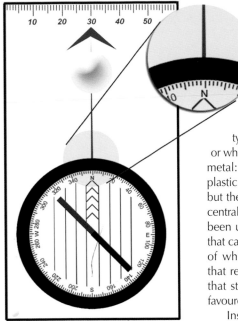

7.3 If you have a compass with the divisions of the degree of scale too far away from the direction of travel arrow, you'll have problems reading the bearing accurately!

a crucial part of the compass that will point you in the direction that you'll need to take when walking on a bearing.

The compass housing is another essential bit. If you don't have one on your compass, it ain't a compass! Inside the housing sits the compass needle, typically red at the north end and black or white at the other end. Not all needles are metal: some of the more modern ones are plastic. Hang on, plastic isn't magnetic – true, but the small bar magnets either side of the central pivot point are. This arrangement has been used very successfully for compasses that can be used over the whole globe (more of which later) and for those compasses that require a stable needle or at least one that stops swinging quickly, such as those favoured by competition orienteers.

Inside the housing, as well as the needle, is a liquid that slows down or 'dampens' the needle's movement. If you've ever had a compass that has leaked you'll appreciate that this liquid is necessary. Without it, the needle swings back and forth for ages. Compasses do sometimes develop air bubbles in this liquid. This may be caused either by a leak in the housing or a change in air pressure caused by high altitude. If the bubble is small and not affecting the swing of the needle, you need have no cause for alarm. However if the needle is affected, it's time for a trip to the shops.

The liquid itself is white spirit, not water as the iron needle would rust, but inside the white spirit on a decent compass is an antistatic chemical that prevents the build up of static. Think about it, you probably tend to wear fleece or at least polyester clothing, and your lovely plastic compass, if it rubs against your clothes can build up a static charge. This would cause your compass needle to freeze and not to point north which could lead to serious navigational problems. A decent compass will be equipped to stop this happening.

The needle is also important. I see some pretty cheap and nasty compasses on the courses I run. There are usually lots of things wrong with them but the thing they usually have in common is that the quality of the needle and its pivot point look appalling; the needle looks like it wouldn't take much for it to fall off. Compare that with the needle on a Silva compass and you'll see the difference. Silva use an industrial sapphire to ensure the swing of the needle is clean and efficient. Silva compasses also have the chemical that prevents the build up of static on the needle as you pull it in and out of your pocket.

Underneath the needle lie the orienting lines, a technical term that refers to the parallel lines that allow you to line up the compass housing with the grid lines on the map. The two central orienting lines may either be drawn as an arrow (**housing arrow**) or marked by two blobs of luminous paint. The arrow (or blobs) point to the north mark on the edge of the compass housing. Around the rest of the housing edge are the other cardinal points and smaller sub-divisions. The ideal sub-division is 2°. If your compass has anything greater than that it's not accurate enough and you need to replace it.

You should also be able to read the degree scale around the housing easily. When taking a bearing you read off against the direction of travel arrow, and so it is easier if the divisions are on the outside of the compass housing. Some compasses have the 360 divisions on the inside of the compass housing, away from the direction of travel arrow, making reading the bearing more difficult (Figure 7.3). At this stage stick with what you have but if, as the following chapters progress, your compass becomes tricky to use accurately, think about purchasing a new model.

You may see compasses that are divided into 'mils' (a military scale). For military purposes mils are more accurate than degrees, since there are more mils to a circle than degrees. For the purposes of walking and other hill sports, degrees are perfectly acceptable. In the UK there are 6400 mils in a circle, so 1° is approximately 17 mils.

All these elements of a compass should be contained within a clear plastic base plate, which should fit comfortably in your hand. Base plates come in different sizes and you should choose what you find comfortable. There should also be a way of attaching the base plate to a string or lanyard.

## EXTRAS

So now you know what a compass should have as a minimum. However, there are additional elements that are more or less useful: some compasses have Romers, which

*A marching compass*

were mentioned in Chapter 4; others have a triangle and circle stamped out of the base plate. (These are used for the sport of orienteering and are unnecessary for walkers. However, orienteering is a worthwhile sport for gaining navigation practice so they may not be entirely superfluous to you.) You may also find your compass has small silicon feet that help to stop it sliding across the map. Great if you have them but otherwise they're not worth worrying about.

One additional feature you may discover is a small screw on the housing. This allows you to adjust the compass to take into account the magnetic variation. My suggestion is that you should leave this screw untouched. You'll discover why when magnetic variation is elaborated on in Chapter 8.

*A protractor compass*

## TYPES OF COMPASS

There are various makes and types of compasses but generally you get what you pay for. If two compasses have the same features and one costs £10 and the other £2.50, you'd suspect that the £10 one is better, more robust and probably more accurate. However, if two compasses from the same manufacturer are priced differently the more expensive one probably just has more features. There are a variety of different types of compass, and each has its own particular use. Occasionally you meet people who still have their old **marching compass** from their days of military service. They pull them out proudly, and why not? However, being told to march on a compass bearing by an officer is one thing, but determining your own bearing and following that is a totally different matter. A marching compass will allow you to follow a bearing but you can't use it to work one out from the map.

The **protractor compass** looks very similar to the one in Figure 7.1. At first glance it doesn't much look like a protractor (those things you used at school to measure angles) but as you'll discover in the next chapter, you can use a protractor compass to work out angles on a map very easily.

*A sighting compass in action on the hill*

A **sighting compass** also allows you to follow a bearing accurately. Here a mirrored lid sits over the compass housing when the compass is not being used. When you are walking on a bearing, you angle the lid so that when the compass is held up at eye level, you can see both the compass housing, in the reflection, and the landscape ahead of you through a small sighting point.

Another type is the **prismatic compass**. This looks and operates in a similar way to the protractor compass; the only difference is in the compass housing. Inside the rim sits a small prism that, when held up to the eye, allows you to see a compass scale which is divided into single degrees.

These last two compasses are more accurate than a conventional protractor one. We'll look at holding a compass in Chapter 9 but, generally, while a protractor compass is held at belly button level, the sighting and prismatic compasses are held at eye level. The prismatic is held next to the eye which makes it supremely accurate for taking and following bearings. A sighting compass is held away from the eye a little which makes it less accurate. I do love my prismatic compass but at £70 a pop, it's probably a bit over the top for a beginner. You can also buy **electronic compasses** (different from GPS devices). I don't have a great deal of experience of these and wonder why one would buy an electronic gizmo that relies on batteries and dislikes getting wet when you can get a small piece of plastic that can get as wet as it likes and doesn't need power to make it work. Perhaps I've missed something but you can't even take a bearing on a map with an electronic compass which means you are spending lots of money on something that does less than half than what a conventional compass does!

*A prismatic compass and how it is held when you're about to walk on a bearing*

*An electronic compass –
do we really need these?*

There are other types of compass too. Some have a swinging needle inside them that enables you to read the angle of dip in rocks; great for dinner parties but not an aid to walking! Others are designed for competitive orienteering and have a small thumb loop to make holding the compass easier. You can even get Braille compasses and compasses for Muslims that indicate where Mecca is.

## GLOBAL COMPASSES

Earlier in this chapter I mentioned a compass that uses small bar magnets either side of a plastic needle. This was designed so that it can be used around the world. This needs further explanation, having been the undoing of many a good navigator.

*A thumb compass is
designed for the orienteer
and not the walker*

*I may have had the wrong compass for New Zealand, but at least the view was good! Lake Wakatipu in New Zealand.*

I was once on the top of a mountain in New Zealand with a group of walkers. We were having a rest and one of the group asked me what another mountain was called. As I had never been there before I didn't know, so I decided to use my compass to identify it by pointing the direction of travel arrow at the mountain and reading the bearing from the compass and applying it back to the map. (You'll discover more about this later on.) I duly adjusted the compass for the magnetic variation but just couldn't identify what this mysterious mountain was. I was under pressure: there was a crowd around me, so I tried it all again and then again. Suddenly it dawned on me, I was using the wrong compass. I should have been using a southern hemisphere compass and not my northern hemisphere one.

*7.4 The MN indicates this compass is designed for the bulk of the northern hemisphere*

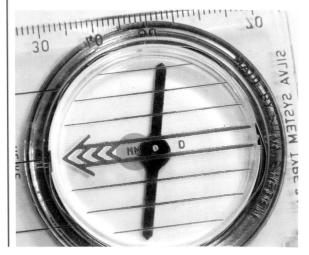

98

Figure 7.4 shows the base of a Silva compass built for use in the northern hemisphere. The letters MN indicate that it is for use in the magnetic north zone. Figure 7.5, taken from Silva's compass catalogue, shows three different balancing zones. These zones require different compasses because of the angle of magnetic inclination. If you suspend a bar magnet from a string allowing it to come to rest naturally, it will not necessarily lie horizontally. The angle it lies at is called the magnetic inclination and will vary depending on where you are in the world and its relationship to magnetic north (the point to which compass needles point, currently in north-eastern Canada). Most compasses are made for just one zone and my problem in New Zealand indicates why you need a different compass depending on where you are. Here, the

*7.5 Silva uses three magnetic balancing zones when building its compasses © Silva Ltd*

*7.6 As the needle is plastic, the small metal piece does the work and swings through the hole in the needle to cope with different magnetic inclinations*

needle, balanced for magnetic north, was actually inclining at the magnetic south inclination. It was unbalanced and scraping round the base of the compass housing, and because it couldn't swing properly, it wasn't showing the correct bearing!

Different compass manufacturers have developed their own solution to the requirement for global compasses. Or you could just buy a new compass when you get to the place where you want to use it.

## BEWARE THE NON-COMPASS

Over the years I have amassed a fine collection of cheap and nasty compasses. They all vary in one way or another but there is a unifying factor – cost. The cheapest Silva compass at the time of writing is £16 – the Field 7. It's a fantastic little compass which has served me well over the years made to the same standards as Silva's more expensive ones.

The rest of the motley collection I have all cost considerably less than that and most are unbadged. Who in their right mind would put their name on something that is so poorly built and in some cases unable to take or follow a bearing with? Some compasses make it difficult to read a bearing, some have two 360° scales which add to the confusion, some have no direction of travel arrow, some look like the needle is going to fall off.

Buy a compass with the name Silva, Suunto or Recta on it and you can't go far wrong (as long as you read on and discover how to use it properly!).

## PERSONAL MAGNETISM

Before finishing this chapter, just a few words of warning. A compass relies on a magnetic needle and many objects will affect it. Zips on jackets, cameras slung around your neck, mobile phones and watches can all affect your needle and send you off on the wrong bearing.

On one occasion a woman complained that her compass needle just wouldn't settle down. The normal culprits were eliminated – no camera and a plastic zip. I was flummoxed! After a while a thought came to her: 'I'm wearing a wired bra.' She was right. The wire inside the bra had its own little magnetic field and was confusing the needle. As she wouldn't remove the bra she had to hold the compass further away from her chest than I'd normally advise. Test your walking gear by holding your compass to various suspect parts. If the needle is affected you'll need to compensate by holding it away from you.

Certain rock types also can affect the needle. Rocks that are high in iron will probably give you a false reading as they would have been laid down when magnetic north was in a different point to its current one. This will have the effect of pulling your needle away from the current magnetic north, especially if the localised magnetic field is strong. The Isle of Skye is renowned for this, although opinions differ as to how much this does affect the needle.

*Fiordland National Park, New Zealand*

In the next chapter there is more detail on compass use and in particular how to read them.

## Key Points

- Ensure your compass has a needle, housing, orienting lines and direction of travel arrow as a minimum.

- The compass divisions should be a maximum of 2° and should lie next to the direction of travel arrow.

- Replace a compass if air bubbles in the housing affect the swing of the needle.

- Marching compasses can't be used to read bearings from maps.

- If walking abroad, take a compass designed for the region you are going to.

- Beware of metallic objects nearby, or on your clothing that could affect the needle.

# WHAT DO WE MEAN BY A BEARING?

## IN THIS CHAPTER YOU'LL LEARN

- about taking bearings
- about the importance of accuracy
- what magnetic variation is
- why magnetic variation is important
- how to alter your compass so you can walk on a bearing

# Chapter 8

Cast your minds back to school maths lessons. Remember the protractor? That little half circle with angles marked on from 0 to 180°? Hours were spent working out the angles of various shapes, drawing equilateral triangles and performing other exciting geometrical exercises. Didn't we all say to ourselves, what possible use would this have in adult life? If only those maths teachers had put a practical slant on the whole thing, this part of the chapter wouldn't require writing.

A bearing is simply the angle (x) between north (N), where you are (A), and where you want to go (C) (Figure 8.1). Whip out your old school protractor and measure the angle. You should find that the angle NAC (x) = 30°. So in principle, if you wanted to walk from A to C you'd walk on a bearing of 30° by turning your compass housing to read 30°. A few stages have been missed out but this gives you the idea. Let's get a tad more complicated.

Figure 8.2 is a simple map. You are at A and want to get to B. To work out the bearing you could use your protractor again, but you can also use your compass as a protractor. Before you do, estimate what you expect the bearing to be. You don't have to be too accurate; between 0 and 90° is sufficient. Once you have taken

*I am not lost; I just don't know where I am right now.*

Lene Gammalgaard (first Danish woman to climb Everest) on being lost on the South Col

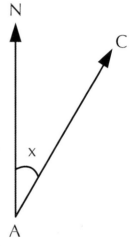

*8.1 A bearing is the angle between north, where you are and where you want to go (NAC or x)*

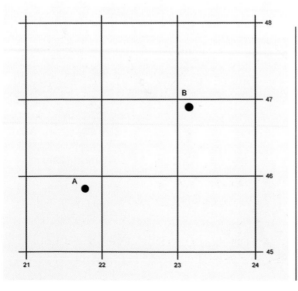

*8.2 Your task is easy: to get from A to B*

an accurate bearing, compare it with your estimate. If the two are very different you've done something wrong and need to take the bearing again.

Let's break down the stages into three simple steps.

1   Place one of the long edges between the two points, making sure the direction of travel arrow is pointing towards B. (There are times when using one of the parallel lines printed on the base plate, rather than the edge, make taking a bearing much easier, especially when the object that you're going from and to is tiny on the map.

2   Then turn the compass housing so that the housing arrow is pointing to the top (north) of the map and the orienting lines are parallel to the vertical grid lines (as in Figure 8.3).

3   Once you have done this, read off the bearing on the compass housing next to the direction of travel arrow. Some compasses have a white or black line underneath the figures which is an extension of the direction of travel line and makes the bearing easier to read.

I told you it was easy. Just three simple steps and you have taken a bearing from the map. When you are using your compass it is important to be as accurate as possible: cut down on the errors now and you will reduce the risk of getting lost later. I often hear beginners say 'It's about 25°.' The word 'about' smacks of inaccuracy. Get it spot on.

*8.3 Your compass is acting as a protractor measuring the bearing*

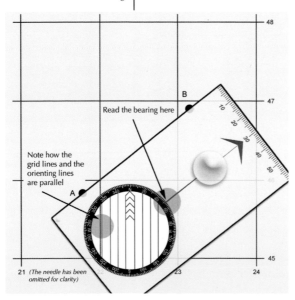

21 *(The needle has been omitted for clarity)*

In the example in Figure 8.3 the bearing is 52°. Do you get the same result? The next stage would be to walk on your bearing with the compass, but we'll save that for later. For now, measure the bearings between the various dots in Figure 8.4a and fill in the table. Compare your results with the completed table at the end of this section (8.4b).

A few things occurred to me while I was filling in the table. First of all, if your bearings are drastically

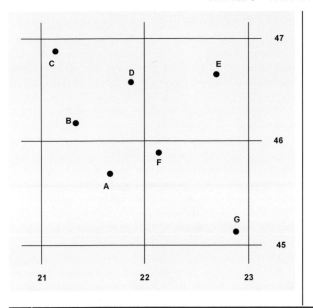

| | TO | | | | | | |
|---|---|---|---|---|---|---|---|
| | A | B | C | D | E | F | G |
| **A** | - | | | | | | |
| **B** | | - | | | | | |
| **C** | | | - | | | | |
| **D** | | | | - | | | |
| **E** | | | | | - | | |
| **F** | | | | | | - | |
| **G** | | | | | | | - |

FROM

different from mine you may have fallen into the trap that most beginners stumble into at some stage. If you were taking the bearing from, say, C to D, did you have the direction of travel arrow pointing from C to D? If not, and it was pointing from D to C, your bearing will be 180° out.

The other basic error that many people make happens when they turn the compass housing. Did you ensure that the housing arrow was pointing to the north of the map? Again, if you didn't your bearing will be 180° out. If you make both errors together, your bearing will be right but I don't recommend this as a technique.

*8.4a Take the bearing between the various dots (keeping north pointing to the top on your compass!)*

But what if your bearings were only a few degrees out? Errors will creep in here if you didn't run the edge of your compass through the middle of each dot, or if your housing arrow wasn't quite parallel to the vertical grid lines. Accuracy is, as ever, important. When I was working out the bearings I had a few problems because I was using a compass with a short base plate. The side of the compass wasn't long enough to stretch between some of the points (C to G for example). This is quite a common problem but is easily solved. Use something that is long enough (a notebook or ruler) and lay your compass along this longer edge.

However, if you consider that the distance between C and G on Figure 8.4 is 9.8cm, this is the equivalent of 2km 450 metres (remember 4cm = 1km) on a 1:25,000 map. A navigation leg of that length is highly likely to lead to errors. Navigating on a bearing takes a great deal of concentration; doing it for this distance is hard work.

Did you notice something else? The difference between the bearing from say A to F and F to A is always 180°; it's an obvious point that many walkers miss. There are, after all, 360° in a circle, so if you walk in the opposite direction to your original one, you're bound to be 180° different. However, when beginners are asked to do the exercise you have just done, many will measure the one bearing and measure the opposite one again rather than doing the maths.

*8.4b And the answer is...*

| | | TO | | | | | |
|---|---|---|---|---|---|---|---|
| | A | B | C | D | E | F | G |
| A | - | 325 | 335 | 13 | 47 | 67 | 113 |
| B | 145 | - | 344 | 53 | 71 | 110 | 123 |
| C | 155 | 164 | - | 113 | 98 | 135 | 135 |
| D | 193 | 233 | 293 | - | 87 | 157 | 144 |
| E | 227 | 251 | 278 | 267 | - | 215 | 172 |
| F | 247 | 290 | 315 | 337 | 35 | - | 135 |
| G | 293 | 303 | 315 | 324 | 352 | 315 | - |

(Row labels A–G on left are under the heading FROM)

## THE IMPORTANCE OF ACCURACY

Let's consider the need for accuracy. When you are working from a map, you need to be as accurate as possible locating the features you are navigating to and from. Figure 8.5 shows an area of moorland in the Peak District. Experience of playing around here with a compass has

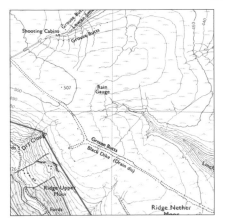

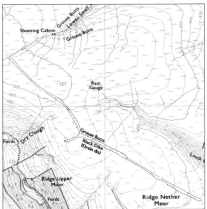

revealed some interesting facts. Take the rain gauge, for example (the remains of a 4ft-high tube of copper). When this book was first published there was no dot or symbol on the map to suggest where it was but the latest edition has a dot (Figure 8.5). Who says the Ordnance Survey don't respond to public pressure? In another book I highlighted another discrepancy between the map and the facts on the ground, and the OS corrected that particular discrepancy but failed to correct the many others outside the area of my map extract. The power of the written word!

Then there are the two shooting cabins. These are clearly located next to the words as two little squares beside the stream. Where there are symbols on a map, make sure that you navigate to these and not to the words!

Other features on this extract (like the stream junctions, the north-western end of Black Dike and the wall ends) are easier to find. When you are taking a bearing, think carefully whether you are navigating to an actual feature or just a representation of it. How about the 507m spot height? Try navigating here and you'll have a challenge. You'll need to start from a known point, but what are you looking for? Being a spot height, you would expect it to be located at a high point, but actually locating this on the ground is not easy. The contours suggest that the ground is gently rising, and not a steep, obvious hill. When you actually get there, it is difficult to decide whether one piece of moor is higher than the next.

Before moving on, let's recap the three steps to taking a bearing.

*8.5 The map on the left appeared in the previous edition of this book. The extract on the right is from the updated map and shows the location of the rain gauge with a small black dot!*

*The elusive rain gauge: would you be able to navigate to here?*

1 Place the edge of the compass on the map between where you are and where you want to go, ensuring the direction of travel arrow is pointing in the right direction.

2 Turn the compass housing so the north arrow is pointing to the top of the map and the orienting lines are parallel to the vertical grid lines.

3 Read off the bearing against the direction of travel arrow.

## MAGNETIC VARIATION

So far I've kept things simple. You've been taking bearings from the map and preparing to walk on the bearing to find another feature. However, there is one more step to take: the alteration of your bearing to account for the magnetic variation. An explanation is needed.

Imagine sitting in the hot seat of the BBC's Mastermind. 'So your speciality subject is North. How many norths are there?' There's a tense silence as you ponder. You draw breath and reply 'One, obviously!' Wrong. There are three norths! The first is the one that Winnie the Pooh found – the North Pole: the north around which the earth spins; the second is the north that the vertical grid lines on your map point to (grid north); the third is magnetic north: the north that magnetic items, such as a compass needle, point to.

The first north (sometimes called true north) is permanent, unless the earth spins off its axis, and is irrelevant as far as walkers are concerned. The second is an artificial north created when the first grid system was drawn over a map (you'll recall Figure 4.4); the vertical grid lines all point to grid north and we all remember from school that parallel lines meet (in infinity – grid north), as do the one kilometre lines that are on your map.

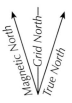

The three norths as shown on the OS Explorer 392 map

The third north (magnetic north), just to make life more interesting, changes over time and because it is a discrete point on the globe, will vary depending on where you are. Magnetic north is currently somewhere in north-eastern Canada and is slowly moving east. Magnetic variation (MV) is the difference between grid north and magnetic north. It will vary depending upon where you are on the globe. In 2012 the magnetic variation for the Peak District was 2.5° west; when I first began to run map and compass courses the magnetic variation was 7° west.

There are some who ignore the effect of the MV when they're teaching bearings – a difference of 2.5° in the Peak District is hardly great after all. However, I always recommend that you do take into account the MV for a couple of reasons. Imagine navigating in a thick mist without considering the MV. Figure 8.6 shows that over a kilometre you would be around 50m off course with an MV of 2.5°. The second reason relates to the fact that the MV varies considerably depending on where you are in the world. If you forget about the MV, then navigating on New Zealand's South Island, for example, where the MV is around 25° east of grid north in Dunedin in the south of the South Island you will stray very quickly with possibly serious consequences.

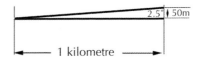

*8.6 A 2.5° error over a kilometre will lead you 50m off course*

## Don't Fiddle

In the last chapter it was mentioned that some compasses have a little screw on the housing that allows you to permanently alter the compass for the MV. You can perhaps see why this is best left unused now. With MVs varying both in time and space, putting it out of your mind by pre-setting it on your compass could lead to problems with accurate navigation when you go to a new location.

## Identifying Magnetic Variation

So how do you identify what the magnetic variation is? Simple: look at the key of your map. The MV for Snowdonia in 1999 was 4°, but a glance at one of the latest Snowdonia Explorer maps reveals the following sentence under the heading 'North Points'. 'At the centre of the E and W sheets true north is 1°27' and 1°42' east of grid north respectively. *Magnetic north is estimated at*

*50m error in a mist this thick this would be serious*

*1°57' and 1°49' west of grid north for July 2010.* Annual change is approximately 09' east' (my italics). Remember there are 60' in a degree. Ignore the first sentence; the second is the important one for walkers.

Let's work through the above example and see what you have to do with these figures. First, as I said, ignore the first of the above sentences as this relates to true north. The second sentence gives two figures here (1°57' and 1°49') as the difference between magnetic north and grid north because it is a double-sided map. So taking those two figures average them which gives is 1°53' and then round it off to the nearest half a degree (which is the level of accuracy that you can alter your compass by) giving us 2°. So the magnetic variation, the difference between grid north and magnetic north for July 2010 is 2° W.

Look on the key of an up-to-date map before you head out for the hills and be aware of the magnetic variation and apply it when taking bearings.

As you might also expect there's a website which will also give you the magnetic variation. Go to www.nearby. org.uk, where you can enter a postcode, grid reference (don't forget the grid letters) or latitude and longitude and it will translate your entry into any number of locational references. There is also a link to calculate the magnetic variation for that location which forwards you to the British Geological Society's website. (Beware: geologists, and this site, use the word 'declination' which is actually the variation between true north and magnetic north. The difference between true and grid north (in the UK) is very small – so you can safely use this figure.)

### Altering your compass

To return to compass bearings: you've taken your grid bearing and want to walk to your next destination. First remember this saying:

*From Grid to Mag, add. From Mag to Grid, get rid.*

This is intended to help you remember that if you have read a bearing from a map (grid) you must add the magnetic variation onto your bearing, physically moving the compass housing round, adding the required amount. By doing this you now have the magnetic bearing instead of a grid bearing. Say the MV is 2° west and the grid bearing is 120°, you add the MV onto the compass bearing to get the magnetic bearing of 122°. This assumes that magnetic

*Map reading on the edge of Kinder Scout*

north is west of grid north. If it is east, as it is in New Zealand or on the West Coast of the US, you need to subtract the MV. You are now ready to walk on your bearing.

I see the next chapter approaching, but before it arrives, let me stress the second half of that mnemonic – 'Mag to Grid, get rid'. Later in the book you'll learn about taking a bearing from objects on the ground and applying it back to the map. If you do this you must subtract the MV from the magnetic bearing to get the grid bearing – 'Mag to Grid, get rid', but enough of that for now. Get a cold cloth, lay it on your forehead and lie in the shade for a while. Only then will it be time for Chapter 9.

## Key Points

- A bearing is an angle between north, where you are and where you want to go.
- Accuracy is important when taking a bearing from a map.
- Ensure you have the direction of travel arrow pointing to where you want to go.
- Ensure you have the housing arrow pointing to the top of the map.
- Always adjust your grid bearing by the magnetic variation (MV) before you walk on the bearing.
- The magnetic variation can be found in the key of most walkers' maps.

# WALKING WITH YOUR COMPASS

**IN THIS CHAPTER YOU'LL LEARN ABOUT**
- walking on a bearing
- holding the compass properly
- the need for accuracy
- back bearings
- simplifying your navigation
- aiming off

# Chapter 9

Having sufficiently rested, you are now ready to walk on a compass bearing. In the last chapter you learnt how to take a bearing from the map and adjust it for the magnetic variation. You are now halfway to being able to use a compass properly.

Let's recap. You have just taken a bearing from a map. You've added the MV and now want to walk on the bearing to your destination. To do this, without touching the compass housing, rotate the whole compass so the housing arrow and the red (north) end of the needle coincide, as shown in Figure 9.1.

*When two paths open up before you, always take the hardest.*

from the film 'Himalaya'
by Eric Valli

## WALKING ON A BEARING

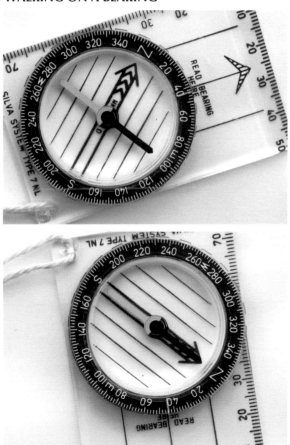

9.1 Turn the whole compass so that the red end of the needle and housing arrow line up

9.2 The correct position for following a bearing

How do you do this on the hill? Photograph 9.2 shows how I advise beginners to hold a compass (unless you wear wired bras!) – anchor the elbows into your rib cage, cradle one hand in the other and hold the compass in the top hand. This way you can only move the compass round if you move yourself. Let me explain why. You are standing on a hillside having taken a bearing from the map. You have added the magnetic variation and are almost ready to set off. Holding the compass as I suggest, turn your whole body round until the needle and arrow are lined up. With the compass anchored to your side in this fashion, if you move your body you are also moving the compass. Even the fine adjustments at the end must be completed by moving your whole body. Then your nose, toes and direction of travel arrow are all pointing in the same direction.

If you ignore this advice, making a rough adjustment by spinning round to roughly the right direction, the temptation would be to twist the wrist for the final adjustment. Fine in theory, but the nose and the toes aren't lined up with the direction of travel arrow and following an accurate bearing is then more difficult. Remember, cut out all those little errors and you'll be more accurate!

So that's easy. You've spun round, lined up the housing arrow and needle and off you go. Well, not quite. If the reason you took a bearing was to roughly identify a direction, say after a debate about which path you had to follow on the ground, and the bearing pointed along a path, then all you would do is head off along that route.

However, if you were taking a bearing because the mist was down and you were in the middle of Dartmoor looking for a wayside cross, you're still a couple of stages away from starting to walk.

9.3a A reminder: this is what you're doing when taking a bearing

You have the bearing. Let's consider what that means again. A bearing is the angle between north (magnetic north now you've added the magnetic variation on), where you currently are and where you want to go (that wayside cross, for example). You are obviously standing where you are and your direction of travel arrow is pointing towards where you intend to go. You've seen Figure 9.3a before in the previous chapter; wouldn't it be wonderful if these lines went across the landscape! Sadly that isn't the case so you have to imagine them (Figure 9.3b).

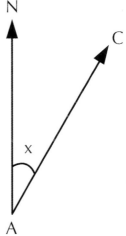

## Looking Ahead
What you need to do is to walk along the line from A to C. To do this, look along this imaginary line for a feature you can identify; this may be a rock, a lump of differently coloured vegetation, something on the skyline or whatever. The feature could be 5m in front of you or 0.5km away: it all depends on the visibility and the terrain. The most important thing is that the feature is exactly on your bearing and not to one side. (You need to make sure the object doesn't move or disappear when you get closer to it – don't use a sheep!)

9.3b You'll need to imagine the lines across the landscape

North

Where you want to go

North

Where you don't want to go

Where you
want to go

*9.4 Don't follow the green
lines*

Figure 9.4 shows your bearing line drawn in red but with a series of green parallel lines. These all follow the same angle but don't take you from where you are to where you want to go. If you're inaccurate when spotting a feature on your line, in a thick mist you could sail right past your intended target.

So identify a feature on your line, put your compass away and walk to it. Take out your compass, identify your next intermediate feature, put your compass away, walk to it and repeat the process until you get to the wayside cross. I'm emphasising putting the compass away because many walkers new to compass work walk with it out all the time, gazing into it as though it was telling their fortune. Apart from being a boring way to walk, it is possible to walk in any direction and still keep the needle and arrow lined up. Put the compass away, enjoy the walk and ensure you are walking in the direction you are intending to! You can concentrate on putting your feet down safely too, especially on rough ground.

## BACK BEARINGS

Congratulations, you have now walked on a bearing! Let me add an extra check. Before you have lost sight of your original departure point, do a back bearing. As this implies, you point your compass back along your bearing to see whether your direction of travel arrow points to where you came from. In this case, however, rather than

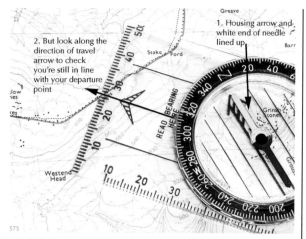

*9.5 Compass set to show a back bearing*

lining up the housing arrow with the red end of the needle, line it up with the other end of the needle. If your direction of travel arrow points back to the departure point you are still on your imaginary line across the hillside. If it doesn't, reposition yourself so that it does and then take extra care from then on. You can only take a back bearing if you can see your original departure point; once you have lost sight of it then you are on your own.

Earlier on in this book it was said, perhaps glibly, that there are only three simple steps involved in reading a bearing. With a couple of extra steps added to the procedure for following a bearing on the ground, navigating with a compass is still a simple process. So why has it taken nearly two chapters to tell you about it all? Fair question, let's sum it all up here.

1 Place the edge of the compass on the map between where you are and where you want to go, ensuring the direction of travel arrow is pointing in the direction you wish to travel.

2 Turn the compass housing so the housing arrow points north and the orienting lines are parallel to the vertical grid lines.

3 Read the bearing off against the direction of travel arrow and add (or subtract if the MV is east of grid north) the magnetic variation taken from the map's key.

4 With the compass anchored against you, turn yourself so that the red end of the needle lines up with the housing arrow.

5 Look along the direction of travel arrow and identify a feature along the bearing you can walk to. Put away your compass, walk to the feature and repeat until you reach your intended destination.

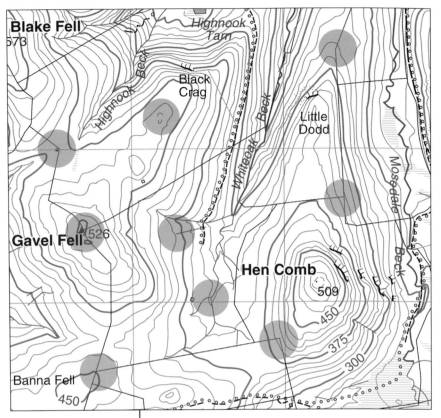

*9.6 Practise taking bearings from the map*

At this stage it would be worthwhile having a practice. Using Figure 9.6 and your compass, take bearings from the various points illustrated. After you have taken each compass bearing, stand up and turn as though you were walking the bearing on the ground. Getting this right indoors makes this easier when you're out on the hill and others are watching you!

## WHAT CAN GO WRONG?

I've mentioned what can go wrong before but it's worth re-emphasising the points at this stage. As easy as the above five steps are, there are a number of mishaps that could occur:

- not placing your compass exactly between where you are and where you want to go
- having the direction of travel arrow pointing in the wrong direction when taking a map bearing

- pointing the housing arrow to the bottom of the map when taking a map bearing
- ignoring or using the wrong magnetic variation
- not ensuring the compass's orienting lines are exactly parallel to the vertical grid lines.

Avoid errors like these and you'll become a safe and accurate navigator.

## POINT TO POINT NAVIGATION

Navigating along linear features is all well and good, but when you start to navigate to point features you'll discover that things take on an extra level of complexity. So how do you do it confidently?

Using Figure 9.7 as an example, imagine you are heading from Madwoman's Stones across to the 590 trig point in poor visibility. If you are even slightly off your bearing you may well head straight past it: the longer your navigational leg, the greater the likelihood too. So what strategies could you employ to avoid missing the trig?

The primary aim of any navigation leg should be to make it as simple as possible. Why make things more difficult than they need to be? So in this case there are a number of options: one could be to take a bearing to the nearby stream and follow it north till you reach the edge path. Then follow the path west, ticking off the streams as you pass them. When you reach the one that's marked A, follow it south until the fork and take another bearing from here to the trig. Doing it this way involves walking on a bearing for only 250m rather than 750m – far better.

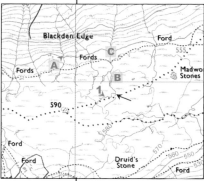

9.7 Make your navigation as simple as possible

A second option would be to take a bearing to the second stream (marked B). It doesn't really matter to where you take this bearing, but common sense would suggest you aim for somewhere just north of the fork in the stream shown by the arrow. Once you hit this stream, turn south along the stream until you hit the fork, then take the northern most arm (stream 1); at the end you only have a short walk along the bearing to the trig (150m).

## AIMING OFF

What you have just done, in fact, is called aiming off and is a very useful technique that you'll find yourself using more and more as your skills develop. You'll have discovered that aiming for a feature and hitting it exactly is hard. If your feature lies on a linear obstacle like a wall, path or stream, then why not deliberately aim to miss your feature? Aiming off does just this. Say you're looking for a sheepfold that lies along a wall. If you aim to hit it but miss, you won't know whether you've got to turn left or right to find it. Instead aim to the right of it, say, and then when you get to the wall, you know you have to turn left, walk along the wall and you'll find the sheep fold. Simple and effective.

Let me give you another example. The stones marked 'C' on Figure 9.7 are on the northern edge path of Kinder Scout. (This is access land, so you can wander where you like.) Again assume you are moving from Madwoman's Stones, but this time heading NW to these rocks. It may be a relatively short leg to do (350m) but you're heading downhill, crossing a couple of streams and walking over rough terrain.

Why not aim to hit the edge path to the right/east of the stones, and then walk along the edge path until you reach the stones 'C'. You don't have to aim too far away from your destination, maybe only 100m to the east. Once you reach the path, turn left and you'll soon reach the stones. (Another method would be to add say 5° to the direct bearing. If you add 5° to your bearing turn left, if you subtract, turn right. In the above example it would make sense to add 5° on.)

Practise aiming off on your next walk and you'll discover how useful it is – especially if you're not too accurate with your bearings!

## Key Points

- When turning your compass to walk on a bearing, turn your whole body at the same time.

- Look along your direction of travel arrow carefully to find a feature on the bearing that you can walk to. Keep repeating the process until you reach your intended destination.

- Back bearings are useful ways of checking that you are walking along the correct bearing line.

- Simplify your navigation legs as much as possible.

- Aiming off is a useful technique to help you find a location on a linear feature.

# CHAPTER TEN

# TIMING, PACING AND OTHER TECHNIQUES

**IN THIS CHAPTER YOU'LL LEARN ABOUT**

- estimating distances
- timing
- ticking off features
- pacing
- navigating around obstructions

# Chapter 10

*If you get lost in an Icelandic forest, stand up*

Old Icelandic saying

A t the end of the previous chapter some methods of making your navigation easier were introduced. In this chapter other techniques to help you avoid getting lost will be considered.

## ESTIMATING DISTANCE

One skill that isn't easy to teach either in person or via the pages of a book is the ability to estimate distances. I can estimate 100m reasonably well having sprinted the distance during my school days; short multiples of that distance are also fairly easy to guess accurately. However, when people are looking across a landscape with distant hills on the skyline, the inevitable question of 'How far is that?' always causes problems. Distant objects can seem quite close at times and further away at others depending how clear the atmosphere is. Long distances are, however, less important for the navigator than shorter estimations. Working out a distance for a particular leg is straightforward on a map. Use the grid lines as a way of estimating, or the scale on your compass for a more accurate measurement.

*10.1 If only the lines were there in reality!*

Being able to look across a landscape and estimate 250m is hard, as is the converse – knowing you've already walked 250m. Practice, as ever, makes perfect and an

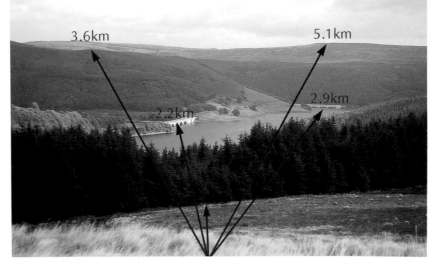

afternoon spent on a hilltop comparing map and ground distances is an afternoon well spent.

## TIMING

Being able to estimate by eye is one thing, but there are other ways of gaining an idea of distance that are more accurate. Timings have been mentioned before in this book when referring to route cards (see Chapter 6). Here's a reminder of Naismith's Rule:

---

**Time Taken = 4km/hr + 1 minute for every 10m climbed**

---

This is a useful guide for planning a full day's walk, but it can also be used to help you estimate how far you've walked on a short leg. For example, let's imagine you are navigating over a stretch of moorland on a leg that is 800m in length; using the above formula you can work out that it should take you around 12 minutes to walk. So check your watch at the start, and when 12 minutes have passed begin to look around for your intended target.

| | |
|---|---|
| 4km | 1 hour |
| 1km | 16 minutes |
| 500m | 8 minutes |
| 250m | 4 minutes |
| 100m | 1.5 minutes |

*10.2 Chart showing the approximate time it takes you to walk short distances. Note the figures have been rounded up to make the maths easier: it's approximate so use it as a guide, not as a rule*

Of course chance may have it that you do arrive in 12 minutes. However, the chances are greater that you won't; delays on the way, breaks to check your map or compass, pauses for breath or the stumbling over a dead sheep or two are inevitable. However, when the 12th minute clicks over you should be aware that you are close to your destination. You may be able to see it but it may require a little searching for. If you didn't keep a check on the time, you may find yourself walking on into the sunset having not seen your holy grail.

Sounds unlikely? Well yes, it does make you wonder whether people would carry on walking way beyond a sensible distance, but it does happen. Novice navigators tend to do it frequently. I recall one wonderful day up on a part of Bleaklow, in the Peak District, with a group of learners. Having asked them to navigate from the end of one drainage dike across to a grouse butt in another drainage dike, the group took a bearing and set off. After a while three of the group stood on a small mound of peat to get a better view across the moor, before heading off again. A little while later, as a group, they stopped again and told me that they were there but 'someone had moved the grouse butt'.

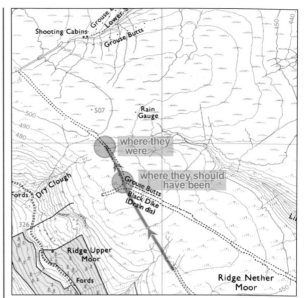

10.3 The route of
the miscreants

Were they sure? Yes, they were, they assured me and showed me on the map just why they were in the right location. The confidence was great to see even if it was misplaced! The little mound they had stood on previously was the grouse butt (albeit in a rather sorry state); they had sailed straight past it and gone much too far. A quick check of the watch would have saved them their embarrassment.

Figure 10.3 shows the route they took. As you can see, the route should have taken them nearly 12 rather than 15 minutes because it was 600m and a 20m ascent. Once their watches told them they'd been going for 10 minutes, they should have checked carefully for the grouse butt.

This story also illustrates that it is very easy to persuade yourself that you are at a point on the map when in reality your location is rather different. The human brain has a remarkable capacity to block out certain aspects of the map that don't fit the ground you are looking at and bend what you can see to fit the remaining symbols.

## TICKING OFF FEATURES

The best way to avoid this is to ensure you tick off features as you pass them. It was suggested before that you make a mental note of the landscape you will be heading over on a particular leg, checking to see if you are heading uphill, crossing any streams or whatever it may be. If you do this and tick them off when you pass, you are helping to ensure that you stay on target. You won't have to study the map suddenly and try matching ground to map. That's already been done.

Certain landscapes make this easier than others. For example a Lakeland valley, with a multitude of streams feeding down the steep valley sides, is easier to keep an eye on than a flat and featureless bit of Dartmoor; having done most of my navigation teaching in the Peak District I'm firmly of the opinion that if you can navigate on moorland, you can navigate anywhere.

## PACING

Another technique you can employ is pacing, and this is a powerful tool. To do this you need to know how many paces you take to walk 100m. If you don't have anywhere with a pre-measured 100m to walk against, look on your 1:25,000 map and find a section of 100m (4mm on the map) that you can identify, say between two walls or streams.

*10.4 It's easier to count every other pace*

**One Double Pace**

That was the easy part. The next stage is to walk it, but rather than counting every step, count every other one (Figure 10.4). By counting double paces you not only save yourself too much mental strain, it also makes the maths easier. I'm lucky with my little legs; I walk 66 double paces to 100m, which neatly means that I have to pace two-thirds of the distance. If you aren't good at on-the-hill mental maths then keep a piece of paper in your map case with distance/paces figures pre-calculated. Mine would look like Figure 10.5.

A couple of words of warning are in order. Firstly, having watched many navigators practise their pacing, I'm frequently reminded of Monty Python's Ministry of Silly Walks. People

| Figure 10.5 distance/pace chart for an average of 66 double paces to 100 metres ||
|---|---|
| Distances (m) | Double paces |
| 10 | 7 |
| 25 | 16 |
| 50 | 33 |
| 100 | 66 |
| 200 | 132 |
| 500 | 330 |
| 1km | 660 |

| Figure 10.6 distance/pace chart for deep heather and rough grassland | | |
|---|---|---|
| Distances (m) | Double paces in deep heather | Double paces on rough grassland |
| 10 | 6 | 7 |
| 25 | 15 | 18 |
| 50 | 30 | 36 |
| 100 | 60 | 72 |
| 200 | 120 | 144 |
| 500 | 240 | 288 |
| 1km | 480 | 576 |

walk so unnaturally when they think about doing it: pace your sample 100m a few times, by which time you won't be as self-conscious! Secondly, as you will doubtless come to realise, pacing along a 100m piece of tarmac is different from pacing over rough grassland or knee-deep heather. However, once you know your basic flat pace, you can then begin to adjust it according to the different terrains you walk on. In knee-deep heather my pacing changes to 60 per 100m as I take longer strides. On rough grassland, the paces rise to 72 as I carefully pick my way through the knobbly tufts (Figure 10.6).

Going uphill make a difference too. When we try this on my courses, some people have to add 25% onto their pacing count, I add 10% and a rare minority have the same stride length uphill as on the level.

A thought may be dawning on you – none of this is very exact, is it? No, it isn't, but, as with keeping an eye on your time, it gives you an idea of the distance you've walked. So when do you use pacing? You may be walking along a path in a thick mist looking for another path that will take you off the hill. Being unsure of the area and how much the second path will be visible, you measure the distance from your last identifiable point

*10.7 Rather than walking through the pond (solid line), pace your way round the pond as shown by the dashed line*

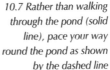

subtract 90°

original bearing angle

add 90°

to the intended junction. Off you pace. When you are approaching the correct number of paces, you will be on your guard looking for the new path.

The same technique could be used along any linear feature when you are looking for a specific point. It can also be used when you are walking on a bearing: you may be heading on a bearing only to come across an obstacle, say a deep pool of water. You don't want to walk through it but don't wish to lose your bearing either. To negotiate this, as in Figure 10.7, first add 90° to your bearing and count your paces as you walk along the edge of the pool.

When you come to the end of the pool, subtract 90°, walking back along your old angle long enough to get beyond the width of the pool. Then subtract a further 90° and walk the original number of paces back onto your old bearing line. You may have also checked, before you started all this pacing, where on the other bank your bearing hit. This gives you an added check that you are back on the right route.

As an exercise, I often send novices off for a little stroll round the hills on a series of bearings and pacings. Figure 10.8 shows what I mean. Three random dots are placed on the map; the distance and the bearings from one to the next are measured before I let my victims have them.

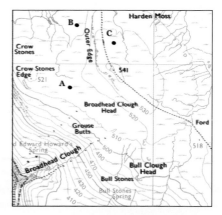

10.8 For pacing exercises any random dots on the map will do, especially if they're not there on the ground, then, starting from a known point (trig point ideally) navigate between them.

Off they go, without a map, starting at a known point (the trig point in this case), pacing the first leg on the correct bearing, repeating the process until they return to the start. It is always interesting to see how close they get to the start. I then suggest they repeat the process but leave their car keys or wallet at the beginning – this promotes rapid improvement!

Another useful exercise is to turn your compass to north, walk a set number of paces and then repeat the exercise facing east, south and west. You should end up walking back to where you left. Try it again with a random bearing (say 53°), adding 90° on each turn. Again you should end up at your starting point.

127

*A suspension bridge, Mustang, Nepal raises pacing problems of a different nature!*

Being able to pace over a short distance will give you more confidence when pacing over longer distances, although care should obviously be taken. Counting is boring and you are more likely to lose track of numbers the higher you get. I'm sure one colleague of mine must have mugged a National Trust employee to get one of those clickers they use to count how many of visitors they've got. He used that to count his paces. I use toggles on an old bootlace tied to my rucksack to count multiples of paces, so I can keep a record of how many I've walked. Pacing is a useful tool, and one worth practising.

## Key Points

- Extra techniques can be employed to help make your navigation simpler.
- Being able to estimate how far you have walked, or need to walk, helps you to stay aware of your location.
- Estimating how long a leg will take you ensures you don't walk too far.
- Ticking off features as you progress ensures accuracy.
- Pacing out a navigation leg also ensures you won't miss your target.

# CHAPTER ELEVEN

# ON GETTING LOST!

**IN THIS CHAPTER YOU'LL LEARN**

- how making mistakes is easy
- how to relocate yourself
- about ground bearings
- about resections
- what to do if you're really lost

# Chapter 11

The man, who makes no mistakes, does not usually make anything.

Bishop Magee

This chapter is one I shouldn't have had to write! If you have followed the previous ten chapters and been out and practised, you should be well into navigation. Getting lost is now a thing of the past and you can mock those incompetents who stop you on the hill and ask where they are. Locationally challenged – not you, eh?

However, reality isn't always quite like that. I've got lost and so have other good navigators. Three of my colleagues were ice climbing in the Scottish Highlands: at the top of the climb they coiled the ropes and set off on a gentle walk off the hill, back to the car. After a while it dawned on them that they weren't going in the right direction. They were staying high and not beginning to descend. Out came the compasses to discover they were

11.1a Point the direction of travel arrow along the path and turn the compass housing to line the housing arrow up with the north end of the needle

180° out! This is easily done at the end of the day when thoughts turn to that restorative mug of cocoa; but it is then when your brain has to concentrate most. Errors when you are tired can quickly become serious.

So accepting that on occasions you may still get lost or at least be temporarily locationally challenged, what can you do about it? Relocate yourself, of course, but how?

## BACK BEARINGS REVISITED

Back bearings have already been mentioned but let me reiterate: when you are walking on a bearing, before you lose sight of your starting point, turn round and line up the white end (or at least the non-red end) of the compass needle with the housing arrow. The direction of travel arrow points back towards your starting point. If it doesn't, then move back on line. Once you have lost sight of the origin, you can't use back bearings.

## TAKING A BEARING FROM THE GROUND

Back bearings are useful to stop you getting lost in the first place, as are other techniques previously mentioned, like ticking off, timing and pacing. The next technique to help you relocate assumes you're following a linear feature. You arrive at a path junction, with two paths roughly heading in the same direction. Which do you take?

- Point the compass along one of the paths (so the direction of travel arrow points along the path (Figure 11.1a)) and turn the compass housing so the housing arrow coincides with the red end of the needle.
- Subtract the MV (magnetic variation) and place the edge of the compass along each of the paths on the map. The correct path will be the one where the direction of travel arrow is pointing directly along it and the orienting lines are parallel to the vertical grid lines. (Figures 11.1b and 11.1c.)

This technique is a useful quick check that you are, or will be, heading in the right direction.

In Chapter 8 you learned the saying 'from grid to mag, add, from mag to grid, get rid'. In Figures 11.1a, 11.1b and 11.1c a magnetic bearing from the ground is read first as the needle is lined up to the housing arrow (the map not being used at this stage) and the MV is subtracted from the bearing to convert it back to a grid bearing, hence 'from mag to grid, get rid'. (This assumes again that magnetic north is west of grid north – see page 117.)

*11.1b After subtracting the MV (mag to grid get rid) lay the edge of the compass along one of two paths (1). Here the housing arrow isn't parallel to the vertical grid lines (2). This isn't the correct path.*

*11.1c Here the edge of the compass lies along the other path (1) and the housing arrow is parallel to the vertical grid lines (2). This is the path you need to take.*

## RESECTION

The next technique is more complicated but only because it involves three steps to locate yourself. The technique is called a resection.

Here is the scenario. You are unsure of where you are.

1  Look around and see three features you can recognise: a trig point, a well-known hill and the edge of woodland. Those three points should surround you (if you draw lines between the three points, you should be inside the resulting triangle).

2  Point your direction of travel arrow at the first feature.

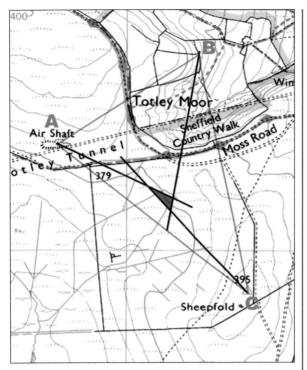

*11.2 You should try to choose three locations (A, B, C) to sight to which, when joined by three lines (in grey), place you somewhere inside the resulting triangle*

3   Turn the housing round so the housing arrow and needle coincide.

4   Subtract the MV and place your compass on your map.

5   Using the identified feature on the map as a pivot point, turn your compass round the point until your orienting lines are parallel to the vertical grid lines and the housing arrow is pointing north.

6   Draw a thin pencil line (in black on Figure 11.2) on your map from the identified feature along the edge of your compass.

7   Repeat this process with the other two features.

8   You will now have three lines on your map, all meeting at a single point or at least making a small triangle. You are either at the single point or, for the sake of argument, somewhere in the centre of the small triangle – the so-called triangle of error (marked in red on Figure 11.2).

The more inaccurate you have been in reading the ground bearing, the bigger the triangle of error will be and the more inaccurate the estimation of your actual location will be too. However, take care over the process and you can be reasonably happy that you are where you think you are.

There are a few points to note. First, if you are not within the triangle made when you took your readings from the three features, you won't, strictly speaking, be inside the triangle of error. If you're a sailor then resection is an important skill to have – to navigate safely into port, but sailors at sea sighting features on land are moving and face the challenge of a pitching boat. To compensate, they've worked out a complicated mathematical formula to calculate their location very accurately. In practice, GPS use is almost universal among sailors. For walkers, however, this level of accuracy isn't necessary. (You're not going to run aground if you get it wrong.) So even if you're not within the triangle created by the features, then continue as if you are.

Bing-bong, your brain should be ringing. If you can identify three features then you can't be lost can you? True to some extent. You will know roughly where you are but not in detail. Doing a resection will give you something approaching that detail.

Using these relocating techniques is all well and good, but having roughly identified where you are it is important to get yourself to a definite position. This means navigating to some feature you can recognise, like a stream junction or a rock outcrop.

However, if you don't know exactly where you are, how can you navigate to a single point precisely? Aiming off, as mentioned previously, would be a good technique to use here. From your roughly identified location, aim off to a linear feature, like a stream. Once there, walk down to an identifiable point like a stream junction. You can then carry on your walk but this time from a known point (Figure 11.3).

## WHAT IF YOU'RE REALLY LOST?

In a chapter on what you should do if you get lost, it is probably a good idea to mention what you should do if all else fails and you haven't a clue where you are. There has been a great deal of research done, principally in the US, into the stages that people go through when they get lost. The American wilderness is much bigger than any wilderness in the UK and you're unlikely to get yourself eaten by a bear if you get it wrong over here but it's interesting to note the five stages. One luminary summed up getting lost quite well by saying 'Being lost is not a location...it is a transformation.' You don't go from knowing where you are to being lost in an instant and it's recognising early on

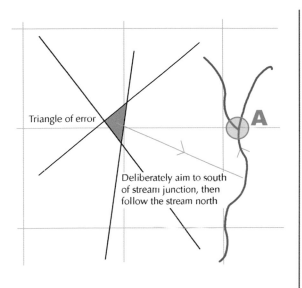

Triangle of error

Deliberately aim to south of stream junction, then follow the stream north

A

*11.3 Navigating away from a triangle of error to an identifiable point (A)*

that you aren't certain of where you are that can save you immense problems later on. So here are the five stages.

1    You deny you are disorientated and press on but with a growing sense of urgency.
2    You admit you are lost and panic.
3    You calm down and form a strategy.
4    You deteriorate mentally and physically as your strategy fails to work.
5    You become resigned to your plight as reality sinks in.
These stages, as I say have been identified in the cases of people in America who get lost, some of whom end up being rescued and the unlucky few who don't and rescuers have to try to piece together what happened.

I have an exercise on one of my courses where I 'encourage' my group to get lost. I don't lie to them, I just evade any question that seeks clarification as to their whereabouts. I've run this exercise for a number of years but the experiences a recent group went through were fascinating, as they carried out the initial stages of the process.

The usual way the exercise runs is that they get to an outcrop of rock on a moorland edge and I ask them to verify that they are where they think they are. Because I have engineered it that they go wrong, they quickly realise by taking bearings from features they can identify around them that they are in the wrong place. On this occasion there was a thick fog and we had around 15m

*Sometimes conditions can change quite rapidly. Ten minutes earlier visibility was excellent. (It was April.) Be prepared to change and alter your route accordingly*

visibility so they had nothing to sight to. I decided to see what would happen if I left the error unchecked and simply asked them to navigate to my next intended location which, naturally, they didn't find because they were starting from the 'wrong' place.

They did everything right to find it; they timed, they paced and they followed a bearing but when they didn't arrive at the spot, the first reaction was 'We can't have gone far enough, it must be a bit further on.' Off they set, as one, looking for the place but as they didn't know where they were, and they were confused by having paced the correct distance, some gave up searching quickly while others rushed further on.

When they'd finally got themselves together again, and admitted they were lost, they started to think logically about what they should do but they were forming strategies based on where they thought they were and not where they actually were. They didn't actually get to stages four and five (deterioration and resignation) – I did feel it was important at one stage to tell them that I, at least, did know exactly where they were. But the experience they went through was immensely powerful and educational.

# Chapter 12

Writing a book like this is a little like compiling a litany of all things that can go wrong on a walk. A few years ago I was leading a training course for leaders and prospective leaders for Ramblers' Holidays. During a session highlighting why walk leaders should be first-aid trained, I drew a stick person onto the white board and asked participants for a list of the injuries they had come across.

At the end of this exercise there was a group of white-faced individuals who looked like they would never lead a group again! The poor stick person had broken every bone in his body and damaged every organ it was possible to damage. The word critical wouldn't have been sufficient for this poor drawing! However, in over 19 years of leading I have only had to deal with a tiny handful of injuries among group members.

The point is that highlighting problems that may occur while you are out navigating does not mean they will happen to you. If they did, I'd give up walking and take up formation crocheting instead!

*The wind and the waves are always on the side of the ablest navigator.*
Edward Gibbon

*Weather like this doesn't mean having to curtail your walk*

It's the role of this chapter to consider what you should do in poor weather or at night. Thick mist has been mentioned before but that is by no means the limit of it: to some extent night navigation has similarities to navigation in foul daytime weather. Foul weather at night just makes the whole experience even more unpleasant!

## AFTER DARK

Let's give the dark brief consideration. Probably as a result of most of us living in bright, over-lit towns and cities, most of us think of night as being dark! It rarely is as bad as all that though. The biggest temptation of the novice is to whip out the torch as soon as the sun looks like disappearing beneath the horizon and use that all the way home. However, if you've ever been out walking at dusk, you'll have noticed that the light takes quite a time to disappear and your eyes adjust gradually as the light fails. It

*Walking in Mustang, Nepal – no problems in these conditions, but what happens if it is misty or dark?*

is surprising how long you can carry on reading your map and compass after sunset. Of course there comes a time when you can't see it, but avoid the torch temptation until you really have to.

The best way to avoid getting into problems is to plan ahead and make sure you're off the hill in time. However, if you are caught out all is not lost. By sensibly applying the techniques you've learned throughout this book you should be able to navigate your way to safety. Remember to keep it simple.

A few years ago I was instructing a group of fairly advanced navigators. We had deliberately planned to stay out after dark. They had planned an elaborate route that needed compass navigation over quite hard terrain. Darkness fell halfway through quite a tricky leg. Their previous legs had all been competently done. This one, however, gave them immense problems as they lost their vision. Eventually they found their point but had a conference and decided they would simplify their route and follow linear features, such as walls, hedges, tracks and streams, for the rest of the walk – eminently sensible. You won't find a mountain rescue team taking a short but difficult route off a hill if a simpler, longer route can be completed more safely. Take the hint from the pros.

Let's summarise a few techniques from earlier chapters that you can still employ if you find yourself walking in the dark.

## Timing

By working out how long a leg will take you, you can keep a check on your location. Time flies when you're concentrating on other things, particularly at night.

## Pacing

Like timing, careful use of pacing can help you to locate features in the dark.

## Bearings

Following a bearing can be easier at night than during the day as you are less likely to be distracted by other features. What do you sight to, though, if visibility is restricted?

- **Stars** If the moon or stars lie on your bearing then walk towards them. Take care, however. Don't follow one for longer than about ten minutes – they move.

- **Skyline silhouettes** As the light fails, the horizon often glows for longer. If there's an obvious feature silhouetted use it. Remember that you must walk in a straight line to be accurate.

- **Torch** Yes, I know I've said don't use them but if you're careful then you can use one to shine along your bearing to help you find features. If there are a number of you, one could be employed as the torchbearer so that your eyes aren't affected as much. If you must use a torch then try closing one eye while you have the torch on. This way one of your eyes will still be adjusted for the dark. Some have a red light setting. These don't destroy your night vision but still allow you to read the map. They do make seeing the brown contour lines more difficult, however. Oh, and a head torch, which leaves your hands free, is better than a hand-held one, too.

Navigating in the dark can be fun and it's probably worth going out to practise sometime (with the usual precautions of telling someone where and for how long you'll be gone). If you know you can do it when the pressure is off, then you'll be happy when you have to do it for real.

## IN THE MIST

Let's turn our attention to navigating in mist. In many ways, this is more difficult than navigating after dark as all reference points will disappear. The techniques explained in previous chapters still work, of course, but there is one technique in particular that works very well in a thick mist (and the dark) and is probably the only sure-fire way of navigating accurately.

### Leapfrogging

Let's just consider again how you navigate normally. You have taken your bearing off the map, you add the MV and then you line up the housing arrow with the red end of the needle. Looking down the direction of travel arrow you look for a feature along the imaginary line and begin to walk along it until you reach your objective. Easy enough, but what happens when you can't see any features ahead because the mist is thick (or indeed because the area in which you are walking is so featureless that nothing is obvious)? If you have a companion, the technique you should use is leapfrogging

Again, this technique is straightforward, and fairly obvious when you think about it. Instead of looking for a feature ahead of you, use your companion as that feature. Here's what to do.

1 Take the bearing from the map, add the MV and line up needle and arrow again.

2 Looking along the direction of travel arrow, send your companion off in that direction (it doesn't matter if your companion doesn't walk exactly along the bearing; it may not even be possible, if the ground is undulating, rough underfoot or boggy).

3 Don't let them walk too far away – you need to be able to talk to one another.

4 After a suitable distance (they could maybe pace out 50 or 100 metres each 'leg'), get your companion to stop and turn round.

5 Look carefully along the direction of travel arrow on your compass. If your friend isn't in line, get them to move until they are.

6 Ask your friend to check by doing a back bearing on you (as back marker, you have the final say).

7 Walk to your friend, while they remain stock still in the correct position. While you walk to them you could count paces too. This way your pacings and bearings are being double-checked.

8 Repeat the whole process until you reach your destination.

With regard to navigating round obstacles on your bearing, if you're leapfrogging with a companion the front person can deviate round the obstacle, taking whatever route they fancy. You then bring them back into line, as before, once they have got round it.

Keeping an eye on how far you've walked is important, especially in a thick mist. Without any other landscape markers to tick off, it is very easy to misjudge how far you've moved.

If there are three of you, with practice it is possible to get a rolling leapfrog going, but this is one for you to discover for yourself once you've sussed the double leapfrog!

It is worth adding a few words of caution here. First of all, all navigators need to have the same bearing on their compass. (I have seen couples who don't!) Secondly, walking this way will throw Naismith's timings up in the air because each leg is being walked twice. This has obvious implications for the overall timings of your intended walk. If you spend all day leapfrogging, your six-hour walk is going to turn into a twelve-hour epic. If you find yourself having to leapfrog for a good part of the day, then you may have to reconsider your plans. (A triple leapfrog can be as fast as normal walking if one member of the group is always walking forward.)

Having said that, there are times when leapfrogging is all you can do. I've had to resort to it on a number of occasions, and even when heading for point features, like trig points, have hit them spot on. Even though I've been doing it for years, I still get a great deal of satisfaction when this happens.

Throughout this book the need for accuracy has been emphasised. The greatest temptation when navigating, especially in poor weather, is to rush your decisions in order to keep moving. However, a rushed decision in this situation may herald a later downfall. Take your time and check your results.

## Key Points

- Navigating after dark is more difficult but many of the techniques in previous chapters can still be employed.

- The most important thing to remember when walking after dark is to simplify the route.

- Navigating in mist can be trickier than navigating at night.

- Leapfrogging is the most effective and accurate technique to use in mist.

- Leapfrogging effectively doubles the time it would normally take to walk a particular route – if you use it a lot you'll have to shorten your route.

# NAVIGATING ABROAD

**IN THIS CHAPTER YOU'LL LEARN**

- about the accuracy of foreign maps
- how to alter your navigation style to allow for less accurate maps

# Chapter 13

There will come a time when you take your newly found navigational skills abroad. As you've seen, the map is the key to good navigation, but therein lies the problem. In Britain, we have been spoilt by the long-running tradition of excellent mapping.

Sadly, even for some parts of Europe, that tradition does not exist, and many maps produced leave a lot to be desired and, in some cases, seem to be more the product of a vivid imagination than fact. So assuming you don't choose your foreign walking destinations based solely on the quality of the maps, what should you do about it?

When I'm walking in snow, I walk with a fairly relaxed style; if I don't know when I'm going to sink into thigh-high drifts and am ready to fall over at every step, it won't come as a shock when I finally do! Using maps abroad requires similar flexible and relaxed attitudes. When you pick up a map, check it carefully before you

*Not all roads lead to Rome.*

(not actually a) Roman Proverb

*Clinton River, by the Milford Track, New Zealand*

have to rely on it. Take it for a little walk and subject it to the kind of careful scrutiny that I suggested in Chapter 3. There is a fence there – is it shown on the map? How do they represent that marsh and stream? Are the footpaths accurately marked?

If the map passes muster you can give it more respect than you can if the level of detail is poor or inaccurate. That doesn't mean, of course, that you can't use it if it is not detailed enough. Just treat it with a pinch of salt. For the past few years I have been over to New England (in the Fall) to walk parts of the immense Appalachian Trail (AT). The maps I used came from the AT Guide, which is divided into sections according to the states they pass through. The Vermont/New Hampshire guide comes with eight maps, all drawn at a scale of about 1″ to the mile. That's not a scale that I would normally recommend walkers using, but when that's all there is...

At this scale my method of navigation changes. With a 1:25,000 OS map, for example, you can tell exactly where you are at any one moment. With the 1″ to the mile maps you have to rely on ticking off features as they are reached; these might be an occasional summit, path/track junction or stream. However, inbetween these locations if people ask where they are, I have to wave my hand vaguely! (It must be said that the route could probably be walked without reference to a map at all – the length of the trail has been well marked with white flashes painted onto trees and rocks at regular intervals. Very effective until you're walking through stands of silver birch!)

## MAPS

One problem that many walkers have with foreign maps is getting used to the way they look and the symbols they adopt. I'll repeat what I said earlier in the book at this stage; if you get into the habit of using different maps in the UK (different scales and OS as well as Harvey's maps), the transition is not quite as shocking when you go abroad.

The availability of maps varies depending on where you are. Remember what powerful tools maps are and why the OS has been for most of its history an arm of the Ministry of Defence. The OS was formed to map Britain as a response to the perceived threat of invasion following the French Revolution. The first maps were of the south coast of England. Some countries still regard their maps as state secrets and you won't get hold of one that is of any use. When planning a trip abroad try some of the

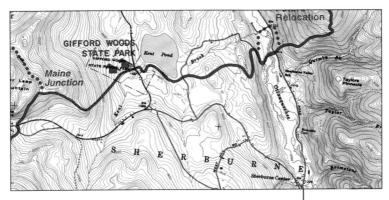

map shops dotted around the country that can get hold of maps from some of the most obscure sources.

The internet is also a good source of information and a direct approach can often elicit a prompt response. I finally tracked down some excellent maps of Nepal via a very circuitous route. I knew that the Finns had been helping the Nepalese with a major mapping project, so an email to the Finnish mapping agency got an email address in Nepal. The next day I had a reply from them giving the physical address of a shop in Kathmandu which sold them. A colleague was furnished with the address and I now have a set of beautiful maps at home, which I use on my trips there. They're excellent by the way!

*Using a map like this requires a different technique compared with a more detailed map © Appalachian Trail Conference*

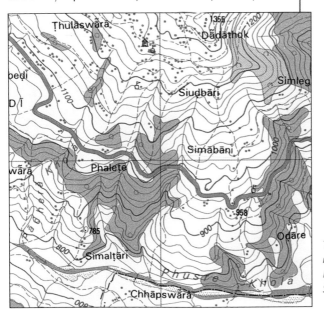

*The superb Nepalese maps © Government of Nepal, Topographical Survey Department*

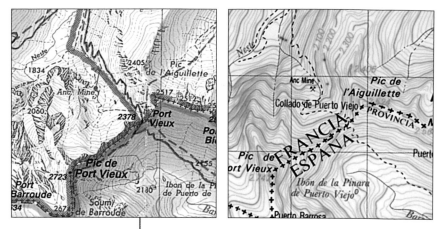

*One place, two maps and very different standards (French map is left, Spanish map is right)*

## Wishful Thinking

Some mapping agencies have a strange habit of including features that aren't there or leaving off ones that are! I remember backpacking in the Pyrenees a few years ago. In France we used and enjoyed the French maps. Over the border, we quickly realised the limitations of the Spanish ones. Compare the two maps above: they are of the same area but the detail on each is very different. The one saving grace was that we had the Spanish maps laminated before we left and they made great sit mats! (Spanish maps are now much improved and are still getting better.)

### Key Points

- It may be a challenge finding decent maps abroad.
- Check how accurate the maps are before you have to rely on them seriously.
- If detailed maps are not available, you will have to adapt the way you navigate.
- Some foreign maps need to be treated with a pinch of salt!

# GPSs AND OTHER TECHNOLOGY

### IN THIS CHAPTER YOU'LL LEARN ABOUT

- GPSs – their limitations and uses
- computer route-planning programs
- the limitations of both

# Chapter 14

*I'm not sure where
we are; the batteries
have gone flat!*

Anon

W hen I'm talking about navigation to walkers, I frequently get asked about GPSs (Global Positioning Systems). Are they any use? Do I use them? When should you use them and when can't you? I've deliberately waited until the end of the book before talking about them for one simple reason: you must be able to read a map and compass confidently before you can properly use a GPS. They are not a substitute for a map and compass.

That said, GPSs are becoming much more common on the hills of Britain. Prices have fallen considerably over the years and they are now also available as a standard addition to smartphones so what was once a toy for a techie with serious money to burn is now a tool accessible to most walkers. GPSs are here to stay, but how good or indeed useful, are they?

## GPS

*Your GPS can offer a host of
useful (and not
so useful) information*

### How They Work and What They Do

Before I answer that, an explanation of what GPSs is probably needed. Without getting too technical, there are networks of satellites circling the earth, each transmitting a weak radio signal which, among other things, includes the time and their location. The Americans have a set of satellites, so do the Russians and Chinese and the Europeans are trying their hardest to get some launched.

Your GPS receiver, or smartphone, has a small aerial that picks up these signals and, using geometrical calculations, works out where you are and, if the unit can 'see' enough satellites, how high you are. The first units could fix on

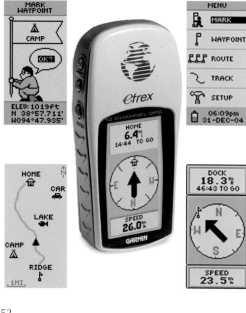

152

*Looking into the Colca Canyon, Peru – when walking abroad with your GPS, ensure the local maps have a GPS-compatible grid system*

a maximum of six satellites; the latest versions can fix on up to 12, making them more accurate and reliable. As well as the satellites, there is now a growing network of ground stations which further increase the accuracy of your receivers; the best receivers are now accurate down to about three metres. So here we have an instrument that can tell you your location and altitude with pretty good reliability and accuracy. But GPSs are designed to be much more than a locating device; they're supposed to be navigational instruments too.

Before I go on, it's time for some honesty. I don't like GPSs. I, along with many others who can read a map and a compass, firmly believe that if you have good map and compass skills, then a GPS is superfluous at best. However in the interests of completeness let's consider just how one can navigate with a GPS. You'll find more detail in my book *Navigating with a GPS: Effective skills for the outdoors* (Cicerone 2008).

## GPS Navigation Skills

Firstly, a GPS receiver will tell you where you are by displaying your latitude and longitude or, more usefully, your grid reference. (Don't forget to reset your GPS for the particular grid system you are in. Most countries of the world have their own grid system – the one for Great Britain is the OSGB36 one.) With a GPS that displays an OS map onscreen you'll get a marker at your location which may also show the direction you are moving in.

So you have your location which you've checked on you paper map you're also carrying but what if you discover you aren't where you thought you were? This does depend on how far off course you are but you'll presumably want to get back on track. Using the data supplied by the GPS, identify where you are on your map and where you want to get back to. If you enter your destination as a waypoint your GPS will lead you straight there. However it is vital that you use your map to check the direct route from your current location to your intended one. A GPS will send you in a straight line between the two points but is the route sensible and, more importantly, safe? GPSs can't interpret the landscape for you so you must do that.

If the route is unsafe or difficult, then you have two options. The first is to use your map and compass skills to navigate a longer, less direct but ultimately safer route to get to your intended location. The second is to enter a series of intermediate points into your GPS to get you back on course.

*'Mine says this, what does yours say?' Wearing garlands isn't compulsory when using a GPS, but the gods may help if you do!*

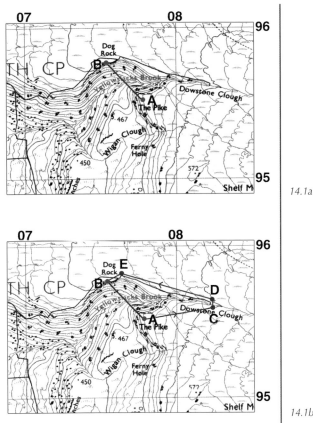

*14.1a*

*14.1b*

Figure 14.1a and 14.1b show this scenario in practice. You might have drifted down the wrong side of the Yellowslacks Brook, checked your location and found yourself at A when you wanted to be at B. Your GPS would send you in a straight line to B which looks like a hard down and then uphill slog to me. My preference would be to take the route C–D–E shown on 14.3b which you can enter into your GPS as a series of waypoints or navigate conventionally with your map skills.

How should you follow your GPS? Should you hold it in your hand and look at it continuously or glance at it occasionally. I see the former quite often on the hill but liken it to the slavish way many people use their in-car satellite navigations systems. By looking continuously at the screen you're divorcing yourself from the landscape you're walking through. Ignoring the landscape and relying on this wee box of tricks with a battery is a dangerous option. The preferred method is to let the GPS give you a broad direction to walk in and then to refer back to it occasionally to nudge yourself, if necessary, back on track. You should also have an appreciation of how long each section is, and have looked at the route on the map and be mentally ticking features off as you pass them.

Many current GPS receivers have the option of using onscreen OS mapping. These are an enormous leap forward from the units of the early days but they still have their limitations. The screen size is the biggest drawback and the second is the ease of zooming in and out and scrolling across the map. At the time of writing I have yet to find a GPS receiver which is easier to use than the mapping software (Routebuddy) I have on my iPhone. But as much as I am a lover of most things technological, a map and a compass is still far easier to use than even the iPhone.

One thing a GPS can do easily is to record the route you've walked. This a useful way of compiling a record of the routes you've walked especially if you upload it to a computer-based digital mapping programme. It is also a good way of reviewing the walk you've done and checking up on any navigational errors you have made.

There are a host of websites, both paid for and free, that have routes you can download for your GPS device, some of which allow you to upload your routes for others to use. Let me throw in a big word of caution here. I've been teaching navigation skills to outdoor enthusiasts for over 25 years. One of the commonest reasons I hear for why people are wanting to learn to use a map and a compass is that they are fed up with getting lost while following routes from magazines and guidebooks. Now in order to be published in a book or a magazine, authors must be authoritative and know the area they are writing a route through. Even then errors do creep in and left and rights get mixed up as well as subtle changes to routes where for example a stile may become a kissing gate which can alter the accuracy of a route description enough to get the user lost.

Enter the plethora of GPS route websites. Who checks them? Who ensures the routes taken are legal and safe? Who checks that the GPS while recording the route didn't have a blip and enter a spurious location. (I was once shown to be 250 metres off the coastal path I was actually walking on once!) I could go on but I'm sure you get my drift. If you want to download the route, check it carefully on your map to ensure it does what you want it to do and goes where it should.

Of course the best option is always to plan a route yourself and upload the route to your GPS. With your route stored you can then use the waypoint locations during your walk. You may want to retrace your steps or return to a location you went to earlier in the walk. By simply scrolling through your stored locations, you can ask the unit to navigate you to that location, or back along the route you've come. You may come across a fascinating area that you wish to return to at some later stage. Again storing the location in your GPS enables you to do it easily.

GPS receivers also help you keep on course when navigating. Assuming your GPS knows where you intend to go to, one of the possible screens on your GPS will tell you whether you are heading in the right direction, giving you a direction to follow if you stray off route. You'll get a read-out of your speed, how long it will take you to get to your destination and a variety of other useful or less useful bits of information. Many units also have the ability to store OS mapping and display them on screen. The photograph on page 152 shows a few of the many screens and facilities that a typical GPS system may contain.

### An Answer to Your Prayers?

GPS receivers are powerful instruments and can lead you round your walk with ease, so, am I just an old fashioned stick-in-the-mud with my objection to them? Well that's for you to decide but remember they aren't infallible. GPSs run on batteries, and although the latest units have a very long battery life, relying totally on one is not wise.

Another reason for caution is again technological: GPS receivers need to be able to 'see' the circling satellites. Woodland and high cliffs are just two reasons why they may not work. If you are using your GPS as the sole means of navigation and your route heads into woodland, you could easily lose your way, and if you haven't been following the map as well, you could be in trouble. They are also computers and we know how reliable computers can be!

But my principal objection is the way they can divorce you from the landscape you are walking through – walking is about being in and part of the landscape, and using a map and compass helps in that process – a GPS doesn't.

### Any Use?

So should you use a GPS? When they first appeared on the market there was a great deal of enthusiasm about them and many thought they would replace the map and compass. Wrong. You need to do the spadework first and learn how to navigate with a map and compass before you can safely head out on the hills with a GPS, and even then you mustn't rely on them 100%.

Let me give you an example. You're on a fell-top somewhere in the Lake District. You spend the day wandering round, letting the unit store where you've been, the weather is good and all is well with the world. However, in the late afternoon you look to the west and see an ominous-looking cloud heading your way. Let's get back to the tent, you say, and set the GPS to take you directly back to campsite in the valley bottom. By this time the mist is in and the rain is pouring, but with GPS in hand you head in the direction indicated by the GPS only to plunge several hundred feet off a cliff top to the valley below. The unit knows where it is, knows where you want to go but doesn't know what the terrain is like inbetween. A glance at the map would have told you about the drop!

Let me tell you a couple of GPS stories. The first relates to the ability of the GPS to store routes. I was leading a navigation group around the Peak District's Bleaklow and I loaded up the GPS with details of the route. Off we went and the unit was working well. It was only when we were heading for a trig point with a fine view that I noticed what it was doing. Around 100m or so short of each of the waypoints I had input, the unit would say 'hang on, we're there' and send me off to the next point. This was before number of satellites a GPS could monitor was increased, however, which may explain the problem.

The second story illustrates how GPS devices can't always be relied upon. I was asked to demonstrate one for a BBC show. A walker was looking for a piece of technology to help him overcome his navigational problems. We met in a pub and I left my GPS on the dashboard to get a fix on where we were. We left the pub and walked up onto the moor for the recording. However, my GPS obviously liked the warmth of the car and refused to acknowledge that we had moved. Fortunately the piece was for radio so I could lie about what the unit was showing us. Never work with children, animals or technology!

So do I recommend GPS receivers? Yes, with the caution I have expressed above. Understand how to read a map and a compass well, and use the GPS as a back-up device for a bit of added fun and information.

I'm writing this in 2012 and already we've seen GPS technology make big inroads into our lives. It would be churlish of me to suggest that the next few years won't see

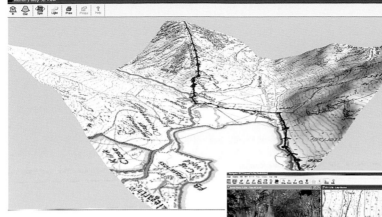

further dramatic developments in the way we use them. How much these developments will affect the outdoor world remains to be seen and whether those developments will alter my view on their role on the hill only time will tell – my eyes and ears aren't closed by any means. I shall just remain a healthy sceptic!

## DIGITAL MAPPING

While we're on the subject of technology, let's turn our attention to the world of digital mapping. The complete OS map range at 1:50,000 and 1:25,000 are available along with the Harvey maps on CD. These programs allow the user to plot routes on screen, to insert waymark points (and make notes about them) and then print them out as a map and a route card (although you'll need to transfer the data into a standard route card format). The information can also be transferred via the appropriate cable to a compatible GPS. Routes you've walked can also be uploaded to your computer and from your GPS.

The various programs differ slightly from each other but all do similar things – you can draw a route onto the map, print out a route card and see the map in 3D. This is a great way of helping you visualise what the landscape will look like and how steep or otherwise your walk is likely to be. You can even change the angle the 3D map is illuminated from, simulating the movement of the sun across the hills and allowing you to work out whether you will you be walking in sunshine or shadow. The programs also include aerial photos so you can see the actual landscape

*Figure 12.2 A sample route on an Ordnance Survey 1:25,000 map shown in Memory Map™ 3D View, Aerial Photo and OS Map.*
*www.memory-map.co.uk*

instead of the map and the maps can be printed out. The software is available for both Windows-based machines as well as Macs and as I've said above are available for smartphones and tablet computers too.

There are also websites that have OS maps viewable online, some paired with the Google Maps, allowing you to compare the map with the satellite images. The functionality and availability of online and offline mapping is changing all the time and at a fast pace, so by the time you read this, things will be very different to the situation in 2012. I shall be watching these developments with great interest.

One exciting project is OpenStreetMap (www.open-streetmap.org). This is a global mapping project that you and I can participate in. Around the world there are thousands of individuals armed with their GPSs recording the line of roads and paths and uploading it to the OpenStreetMap website and essentially mapping the world. With the usual health warnings of accuracy, it shows just how powerful and inclusive the internet has become. There are interesting offshoots as well including OpenCycleMaps. It's definitely one to watch in the future.

However, before I get too enthusiastic let me remember what this book is about – navigation. Digital technology is all very well and good but it does rely on batteries. The quote at the beginning of the chapter is a real one from someone I walked with. (I've called him Anon to save his blushes.) A map and a compass need no batteries or programming ability. If you rely on your GPS or smartphone all day, the batteries may well run down just at the end of the day when you're most in need of good navigation to get you off the hill and to that cup of tea. Always, always, always carry a map and a compass and only use technology when you're thoroughly familiar with both.

## Key Points

- GPSs are highly technical pieces of equipment that tell the able navigator a great deal of useful and accurate information.

- Computer mapping programs can add another dimension to your route planning and navigation.

- Any technology that relies on batteries should be used with care and not relied on exclusively.

- Technology is no substitute for having a thorough knowledge of map and compass skills.

# CHAPTER FIFTEEN

## FURTHER PRACTICE

**IN THIS CHAPTER YOU'LL LEARN**

- how to plan a navigation refresher weekend
- about orienteering as a sport and a way of practising map and compass skills
- about further possible training opportunities

# Chapter 15

*A grapefruit is a lemon
that had a chance and
took advantage of it.*

Oscar Wilde

A book like this has its limitations. For years I have advised folk to go on a course first and then to read a book (now he tells me!), and to a large extent I still believe that's the best way round, although the text you've just read should go a long way to helping you to understand it all, having been written from a very practical standpoint.

However you've come to navigation, you will need to practise your skills. It is no good having spent valuable time learning them only to not use them for ages, discovering what you have forgotten only when it is too late. Why not allocate maybe two weekends a year in your diary to go out with your map and compass and practise some of the things I've mentioned?

Below is a suggested weekend's practice routine. It is not location-specific so can be done anywhere you choose, but I'd suggest you try an area new to you, if for no other reason than to see some more of this green and pleasant land. Try it all with a friend, too, both for safety and companionship.

## A WEEKEND'S PRACTICE
### Day One

**Morning:** spend the morning walking a route that involves lots of footpaths and route choices. Study the detail of the map carefully and compare the map detail with the ground detail. Use a variety of maps and scales.

**Afternoon:** find an area (of access land) that doesn't require you to stick to footpaths, and practise route finding. Use linear features like paths, walls and streams to navigate by. The compass probably won't be necessary all the time, although you may wish to try a couple of practice bearings.

**Evening:** if you are feeling confident why not stay up on the hill into the gathering gloom to get a feel for night navigation? You have obviously told someone responsible where you are going and what you intend to do. Don't forget that restorative lemonade when you've finished too!

## Day Two

Day Two will allow you to use your compass more. Return to your piece of open access land and identify various points as features to try navigate to and from. Obvious point features can be used along with junctions of linear features. Try navigating on your own and then leapfrogging with your partner. Aiming off and back bearings should all be in there. By the end of the day you should be able to set yourself, or preferably your companion, some tricky navigational legs and successfully get there.

## ORIENTEERING

One excellent way to help you improve your navigational skills is to have a go at the sport of orienteering. The word 'sport' may put some of you off, but don't let it. It is competitive, but only if you want it to be. In essence the idea behind orienteering is to locate a series of orange and white flags, which have been placed in attractive bits of countryside. Some mad fools dash around wearing garments that look like nylon pyjamas, trying to complete the course in as fast a time as possible. Others take a gentle stroll as a family group, making it a fun day out. Most of us fall somewhere in between the two.

The great thing about orienteering is that all shades of participation are welcome and there are usually a variety of courses at a variety of standards to suit all.

The first thing you'll notice about orienteering is that the maps are different (see the example in Chapter 2); they resemble the colour schemes used by Harvey's maps and their scale is very different to usual walking scales. However, as I have said throughout this book, getting used to different maps is something every walker should do: orienteering with a 1:10,000 map one week and a 1:15,000 another helps considerably.

## FURTHER TRAINING

Further training in navigation skills is another option. I suppose the ultimate is getting a mountain leadership qualification (summer, winter and then mountain instructor), details of which you can get from the Mountainwalking Leader Training Board, but for many walkers going this far is a little over the top. A more realistic option perhaps is embarking on the National Navigation Award Scheme (NNAS).

The NNAS tries to provide a structured learning programme for navigators of all kinds. It's divided into bronze, silver and gold levels and takes the participant through the various skills needed for good navigation – from close map work and navigation along linear features through to point-to-point navigation and ending with contour navigation.

There are a number of courses around the country (including my own – https://silvanavigationschool.com) and details can be obtained from the NNAS office. What must be stressed, however, is that this isn't a qualification. It's a measure of competence for which you get a badge and certificate at each level; it doesn't qualify you as a navigator.

## WILL THE PENNY EVER DROP?

You're now near the end of the book and if you've read it through and are not in a bookshop flicking through backwards, you will have invested a fair amount of time and effort into becoming a competent navigator. I have emphasised throughout that practice is the key to success and I'm not about to change my tune now.

I have a good friend who, among many other things, is a ski guide, spending weeks at a time on and off the pistes. I remember a conversation with him about skiing and how novices (myself included when it comes to skiing) fairly quickly go from total incompetent to being able to get from the top to the bottom of a slope without falling over. What takes the time is the next stage of going from an inelegant flailing baboon to a graceful and fluent skier. That comes with time, practice and a sudden 'Ahh' moment when it all suddenly clicks into place.

The same thing applies to learning navigation. My students who complete the bronze course suddenly immerse themselves with gusto in the map, smugly sneering at lesser mortals who either don't carry a map or give it a quick glance. Then comes the silver and the student suddenly realises what they're missing in life and that is the compass. Not only do they now understand how a compass works but they also can use it and, boy, do they! Out

*It sounds easy doesn't it, finding one of these?*

*Practice makes perfect*

Tassilaq village, Greenland
– better to be a skilled
navigator before attempting
true wilderness expeditions

it comes at every available opportunity even to negotiate the frozen food isles of their local supermarket!

Now consider our days on the hills when you've encountered someone who knows what they're doing on the hill. Do they slavishly pore over their map or spend their days taking bearings from it and following it on the ground? Let me answer that question for you – no! If I'm not teaching compass use I use mine less than 5% of the time when I'm on the hill, even if the weather is foul. I do use my map but it's a look and then put it away to walk the next leg while mentally ticking off the features as I progress along it. I use the contours to get a feel for the landscape and travel with the ground and not over it. I do study the map carefully and follow a bearing if conditions dictate I need to but I spend most of my walking time doing what I started this game for in the first place – getting out, enjoying the views and the good company I'm with.

If you've turned to this book as a beginner you won't be at that stage yet but the more you do the more you'll find the skills of navigation become automatic and in time you will suddenly find yourself tied to the map and compass less and less. The reference to 'art' in the title of this book isn't accidental. Once you have acquired the skills of navigation there will become a point where you and the landscape you're walking in become more attuned and your navigation becomes more of an art than a science as you feel more in tune with the hills and consider them less something to conquer. That point will come, believe me.

The British countryside is perhaps the nation's greatest resource and one that everybody should have the right to enjoy and appreciate. The freedom to enjoy these areas is not a right that should be taken for granted, as more than a hundred years of access struggles have shown. Some areas should always be limited in access, whether that is productive farmland or precious conservation areas. However, the freedom of the mountains, moorlands, heaths and downs can only truly be gained safely with a thorough knowledge and appreciation of navigation skills. If this book has started you on the road to freedom then it will have done its job. Following Oscar Wilde's comment quoted at the start of this chapter – Don't be a lemon, become a grapefruit. And enjoy it too!

## Key Points

- Regular practice will ensure your map and compass skills are kept fresh.
- Orienteering is a good way to practise navigation.
- The National Navigation Award Scheme provides a structured practical way of developing your map and compass skills.
- The freedom of the mountains, moors, heaths and downs will only be yours once you have mastered the skills of using your map and compass.

# APPENDIX A
## USEFUL ADDRESSES

### Navigation training providers

Details of navigation courses and qualifications can be obtained from the following:

**The Silva Navigation School**
Jaret House
Queen Street
Tideswell
Derbyshire
SK17 8JZ
Tel: 01298 872470
info@silvanavigationschool.com
www.silvanavigationschool.com

**British Orienteering Federation**
8a Stancliffe House
Whitworth Road
Darley Dale
Matlock
Derbyshire
DE4 2HJ
Tel: 01629 734042
info@britishorienteering.org.uk
www.britishorienteering.org.uk

**British Mountaineering Council**
177–179 Burton Road
Manchester
M20 2BB
Tel: 0161 445 4747
info@thebmc.co.uk
www.thebmc.co.uk

**Mountainwalking Leader Training Board**
Siabod Cottage
Capel Curig
Gwynedd
LL24 0ET
Tel: 01690 720314
info@mltb.org
www.mltb.org

**The National Navigation Award Scheme**
32 Stirling Enterprise Park
Springbank Road
Stirling
K7 7RP
Tel: 01786 451307
www.nnas.org.uk

**The Ramblers' Association**
2nd Floor Camelford House
87–90 Albert Embankment
London
SE1 7TW
Tel: 020 7339 8500
www.ramblers.org.uk

### Map suppliers

**Ordnance Survey**
Adanac Drive
Southampton
SO16 0AS
Tel: 08456 05 05 05
www.ordnancesurvey.co.uk

**Harvey Maps**
12–22 Main Street
Doune
Perthshire
FK16 6BJ
Tel: 01786 841202
www.harveymaps.co.uk

### National Parks

**Association of National Parks**
Ponsford House
Moretonhampstead
Devon
TQ13 8NL
Tel: 01647 440 245
www.anpa.gov.uk

# INDEX

# NOTES

# LISTING OF CICERONE GUIDES

For full information on all our
guides, and to order books and
eBooks, visit our website:
**www.cicerone.co.uk.**

# Walking – Trekking – Mountaineering – Climbing – Cycling

**Over 40 years, Cicerone have built up an outstanding collection of 300 guides, inspiring all sorts of amazing adventures.**

Every guide comes from extensive exploration and research by our expert authors, all with a passion for their subjects. They are frequently praised, endorsed and used by clubs, instructors and outdoor organisations.

All our titles can now be bought as **e-books** and many as iPad and Kindle files and we will continue to make all our guides available for these and many other devices.

Our website shows any **new information** we've received since a book was published. Please do let us know if you find anything has changed, so that we can pass on the latest details. On our **website** you'll also find some great ideas and lots of information, including sample chapters, contents lists, reviews, articles and a photo gallery.

It's easy to keep in touch with what's going on at Cicerone, by getting our monthly **free e-newsletter**, which is full of offers, competitions, up-to-date information and topical articles. You can subscribe on our home page and also follow us on **Facebook** and **Twitter**, as well as our **blog**.

**Cicerone – the very best guides for exploring the world.**

## CICERONE

2 Police Square  Milnthorpe  Cumbria  LA7 7PY
Tel: 015395 62069  info@cicerone.co.uk
**www.cicerone.co.uk**